Simulating Terrorism

Stephen Sloan

By Stephen Sloan

A Study in Political Violence: The Indonesian Experience (Chicago, 1971)

Responding to the Terrorist Threat: Security and Crisis Management (coeditor with Richard H. Shultz, Jr.) (Elmsford, N.Y., 1980)

Simulating Terrorism (Norman, 1981)

Library of Congress Catalog Number 80-5937

To my wife, Roberta Raider Sloan, a rare
individual, who has combined her love of
tradition and family with the dedication of a
professional who is leading the way for other women.
May our daughter, Maya, follow her example.

Contents

viii   Contents

Illustrations

Preface

This book is the result of a combination of circumstances, research interests, and personal experiences. It is the end product of outwardly diffuse concerns that I have consciously and intuitively channeled into coherence in the past fifteen years. The work cannot be neatly categorized into a particular discipline because the inspiration and method behind it come from different sources.

In June, 1965, I went to Indonesia to do field work for my dissertation. Getting into the field still remains a vital requirement for my ongoing research and over the years has impelled me to go beyond library resources in an academic setting. Initially I intended to study student indoctrination programs under the Sukarno regime, but on the evening of September 30, 1965, a series of events plunged the archipelago into a bloodbath and forced me to redefine the direction of my research and alter my general views on politics. At that time an abortive coup was initiated by the Communist Party of Indonesia. It resulted initially in the death of six generals. In the reaction that followed, over 300,000 people were killed. While the justification for the carnage was often stated in political terms, many of the murders resulted from religious fanaticism, personal vendettas, and other factors that were only distantly related to the attempted seizure of power in Djakarta. The bloodletting forcefully introduced me to violence on a mass scale. A number of individuals I knew disappeared. I witnessed chaos in the countryside and lost some of the idealism that was common to young graduate students in the early 1960s. I reluctantly accepted the reality of violence in social and political orders at a time when an external conflict, the Vietnam War, was about to lead to confrontations within the United States. The comfortable assumptions I had concerning the ability of both developed and transitional states to resolve issues through compromise were shattered as I watched villages burn in Bali and mobs attack the stores of Chinese merchants in the capital.

Because of the upheaval I changed my research topic. The resulting investigation was an attempt to explain the dynamics of the conflict that ultimately led to the fall of Sukarno. The conclusions were published in a book entitled *A Study in Political Violence: The Indonesian Experience.*

As a result of the research I developed a specialization in the area of comparative political violence. This specialization would take on added meaning in the late 1960s and the early 1970s when violence erupted in the central cities and on college campuses. On a reduced but still frightful scale the Indonesian experience was becoming the American experience. While my university was spared large-scale physical conflict, we came close to becoming a battleground after the Kent State confrontation and the Cambodian invasion. Like so many others, I had a personal stake in the Vietnam conflict when my younger brother was drafted and became a combat infantry soldier in the Mekong Delta. Understanding violence took on a personal significance. Events had demonstrated that violence was not simply what happened to the other person. We were all by degrees potential victims or survivors.

In the academic realm my focus on political violence was part of a broader concern with the study of political change. As a scholar of comparative politics who conducted classes on the politics of the new states, I was particularly interested in the impact of violence on the complex processes of political development and modernization.[1] Consequently I felt most fortunate to receive a Fulbright grant to lecture at Tribhuvan University in Nepal in 1972–73. Throughout most of my stay the tensions related to reconciling a traditional social order with the demands of an increasingly technological universe manifested themselves in political conflict, but the pressures for change occasionally did lead to physical conflict when students and authorities confronted each other in incidents that, ironically, bore a resemblance to what I had left in the United States. The violence lacked the intensity that I had seen in Indonesia, and it did not receive the publicity that accompanied incidents in the United States, but it served to affirm the crucial role played by the threat of or resort to civil strife in politics.

My interest in terrorism per se would take longer to evolve, however. While it was a logical extension of a long-term interest in comparative violence, it would again take field experience to sharpen and redefine my research agenda. I believe that this focus was largely the result of my studies in Israel in the summer of 1975. In that short period I began to appreciate more fully the challenges posed by terrorist tactics and strategies in areas of strife. But the fuller maturation of my interest would evolve more slowly. It was not until I reviewed the horrors of Munich, the incidents of hostage-taking by initially obscure groups, and the skyjackings that seized the headlines that I began to appreciate more fully contemporary terrorism not only as a different type of violence but as a unique form of terror. I recognized immediately that contemporary terrorism is often non-territorial in nature, that the modern-day terrorist engages in operations that are not limited by boundaries or spatial battlefields because the entire world is a target of opportunity.[2] As a result, with Richard Kearney and the members of my seminars on terrorism, I began to analyze systematically incidents of international terrorism.[3]

The resulting studies did provide a series of patterns that apply to incidents of terrorism. Particularly striking is that, in the event of a hostage-taking, the longer the siege continues the greater is the likelihood for survival of the captives.[4] In a war that recognizes no innocent parties, this finding suggests that there are techniques that can be developed to rescue the victims from an undeserved and often fatal punishment. However, it was also apparent that, with the exception of such pioneering units as the Emergency Service Division and the hostage negotiation teams of the New York Police Department, most civilian and military forces had still to develop an effective response strategy to terrorism in general and hostage-taking in particular.[5]

While the data confirmed other studies that recognized the lack of preparedness in meeting the terrorist threat, I felt that I should do more than present our findings at professional meetings or write articles primarily for members of the academic community. In a sense I wanted to get back into the field by operationalizing the knowledge we had gained to assist those charged with meeting the threat of terrorist incidents. Moreover, I was particularly concerned about developing programs that could aid responding forces to develop techniques that would enhance the chances for hostages to survive their ordeals. It was here where, unaccountably, my personal background influenced the conduct of my research.

My family comes from a theatrical tradition. My father's granduncles played on the circuit, and he, a frustrated actor, became a dentist who treated show people. For many years he served on the board of the Friars, the New York theatrical club. My mother also caught the fever. She was a member of a woman's theatrical club called the Troupers. My sister went to the next logical stage and appeared on Broadway and performed on children's shows in the early days of television. My younger brother followed suit. A graduate of New York's High School for Performing Arts, he is still deeply involved in community theater. In contrast, neither my older brother nor I was attracted to the stage. I firmly believe that in my case it was because I lacked talent. Nevertheless, as a teacher I now have a captive audience whose performance I review.

I do not think that my exposure to and subsequent love of

theater was a major reason for my good sense in selecting my wife. But it may be more than coincidental that she also is a very fine actress, a former professor of drama, and currently manager of production for public television in Oklahoma. She has always been the best critic of the simulations I have conducted over the years.

It was therefore logical to me that if, as Brian Jenkins contended, "terrorism is theater," [6] I could relate my love of the performing arts to the data that had been acquired and develop very realistic exercises to help authorities deal with the threat of terrorism.

In developing the simulation technique, we found that the quality of "performance" differed from exercise to exercise. While all the simulations were conducted with a seriousness that matched the challenge, humor at times did intrude to make me recognize that in the final analysis the participants were fortunate that they were not involved in an actual incident. The humor also forced me and others to recognize our foibles. Thus in one simulation my wife was asked to play the role of a nurse who would treat a wounded hostage as part of ongoing negotiation. As she left to an uncertain fate, she made one parting remark, reminding me that if she was not released within the hour I should notify the babysitter. Such are the mundane facts that guide our destinies. In another simulation a rather strident white woman who was ostensibly schooled in the techniques of human relations attempted to win over the terrorists who were led by a black Special Forces captain by "relating to his experience." Toward the end of the discussion she told him that "some of my best friends are . . ." We have captured the reaction to this statement on tape. It contains a wonderful collection of "expletives deleted." But, let me add, this individual might have done the same thing in an actual incident. It is amazing what people will do under stress. Finally, there was the comedic element in the same exercise when a Special Forces lieutenant colonel ordered fifty hamburgers as part of the negotiation for the release of the hostages. Unfortunately, his troops launched an abortive attack, and most of the hostages were killed. The lieutenant colonel was stuck with a tangible reminder of his force's tactical miscalculation.

Such comic releases are necessary on occasion to remind us of our own fallicies and to reduce our anxiety. But the laughter can only be momentary, for in these simulations one cannot play at terrorism because improper training can have fatal results. Yet, if terrorism is a form of theater, it is a new form of theater—the theater of the obscene, where the performance often ends in carnage.

The following study, therefore, is the product of mixed forces, but there is a central concern that has and will continue to impel me to continue my research in the area of terrorism. Despite the rhetoric that has been employed in acts of terrorism, I feel that there is never justification for the murder of innocent hostages whose only "crime" often is that they were on the plane that was skyjacked or walked by the car when the bomb exploded. They have been victims of a new barbarism—guilt by location. In the final analysis the simulations are meant to help keep all of us from becoming victims in an undeclared and horrible war.

Acknowledgments

In the development of the simulations, much as in a theatrical performance, there was a very extensive cast of characters. All of them brought their unique skills to the creation and execution of the exercises in which they participated. I regret that I cannot acknowledge all of them. The following individuals are representative of all those who cared about doing more than simply talking about terrorism.

Thanks are due the following members of the Academic Community: Professor Richard Kearney, who worked very closely with me in developing the original studies and who in one instance was a very convincing terrorist; Professor Richard Schultz, who has shared with me a concern for rigorous inquiry into the dynamics of contemporary terrorism; Dean Joan Wadlow, for her innovative program on terrorism; Professor Hugh MacNiven and all my colleagues in the department of political science at the University of Oklahoma, who helped to create an environment where I could do my work.

The following men from the law-enforcement and military professions and their organizations were willing to test their ability to deal with a terrorist incident by participating in the simulations: Chief Bill Jones, Oklahoma University Police Department; Chief Don Holyfield, Norman Police Department; Lieutenant Colonel "Bo" Gritz, 7 Special Forces Group; Chief Carrol Erickson, Minot Police Department; Sergeant Don Green of the 91st Security Squadron, Minot Air Force Base; Major David Howe, 51st Security Squadron, Osan Air Force Base, Korea; and Lieutenant Reike Coppins, formerly of that squadron. I would like to thank them and also Emmet Mitten, Maurice Cummings, and Neville Trendle of the New Zealand Police; Chief John E. ("Jack") Cunningham of the Port of Portland, Oregon, Police and the one and only Richard Piland; Chief Harry Stege and Deputy Chief Bob Dick of the Tulsa, Oklahoma, Police Department and the management and security personnel of the Sun Oil Company; and Major James Fraser of the U.S. Army Military Police School and Lieutenant Colonel Bard O'Neil, U.S.A.F., of the National War College, who granted me an opportunity to assist in the development of their programs.

In the aviation sector I am indebted to Harry Pizer, Chief of Corporate Compliance for Braniff International Airlines, with Lynn Townsley, Joy Hargrove, and William F. Smith, Vice-President, Inflight Services; Ross Anderson, Security and Ground Safety Manager, New Zealand National Airlines; Roydon Sutherland, Security Manager, Air New Zealand; and Douglas Nelms, a former student, a close friend, and one of my best fans.

From the media Michael Boettcher, now with the Cable News Network, deserves a special thanks for covering the story of the simulations; as does Robert ("Carlos") Duncan, an extraordinary author who lived a plot from his books in an exercise.

Others to whom I am grateful are John St. Denis of the State Department, a fine diplomat and an excellent "terrorist"; John Gittinger, who has shared his insights based on experience; Michael McEwen, a "man for all seasons," who brought his diverse talents to the endeavor; and Bob McLain, a good friend and a fine gentleman. And, finally, to all the members of my seminars on terrorism, particularly those who were "hostages" and "terrorists" or took other roles in the simulations, a special thanks for going far beyond the course requirements.

Norman, Oklahoma   STEPHEN SLOAN

Simulating Terrorism

1 Introduction

When a kidnapping takes place on a street in Rome, or when hostages are seized in an Israeli school, the world is both attracted and repelled by the fleeting electronic images of the event that transmitted on the evening news. The inherent drama provides us with a sense of danger. We watch passively without experiencing the fear and pain that grip the victim. The carnage is repulsive, but it is usually edited and sanitized to protect us from the realities of violence. Nevertheless, the assassinations, bombings, and hostage-takings serve as reminders that global conflict ultimately is measured not in terms of relations among states but in terms of victims and personal horrors. Yet, despite the fascination and repulsion often accompanying incidents of terrorism, the global assault on civil order often is only dimly perceived by the potential victims of contemporary terrorism. Often we unconsciously choose to insulate ourselves from the acts of violence that we witness. Intuitively we feel that such acts are not relevant to our experience. The tactics of terror somehow relate only to other people in other places.

Even when individuals grudgingly recognize that they may be potential targets, the temptation still remains to avoid thinking the unthinkable. If one accepts the possibility that he or she is vulnerable, the realization can provoke anxiety in an already pressured society. Moreover, acceptance may be viewed by others as creating an unnecessary burden on those who wish to ignore the grim possibilities. For those who either willingly or un-willingly remain uninvolved and uninformed—even if they may be potential victims—terrorism is primarily an abstraction that takes on a vague meaning between commercials on the six o'clock news. For most of us, acts of terrorism may only dimly enter our reluctant consciousnesses.

Today the threat of terrorism is being treated with grow-ing concern by the law-enforcement community, the military, and executives in the public and private sectors who must be prepared to meet the potential danger. The development of so-phisticated weapons and related hardware, the training of spe-cialized forces in the increasingly complex techniques of anti-terrorist operations, and the growing body of literature on the tactics and strategies of terrorism affirm the sense of urgency among those who are charged with meeting a new and invid-ious threat. Yet, despite all the current activities, the state of preparedness is at best uneven. A few highly touted units are now being modeled after the Israeli commandos and the Ger-man Border Protection Group 9, but in most local jurisdictions relatively unskilled units are responsible for dealing with terror-ist incidents.

The concern over the threat has spread to the realm of policy making and execution. Officials on local, state, and national lev-els are confronted with the task of devising contingency plans to deal with a strife incident. Furthermore, administrators are seeking to refine their "crisis-management techniques" to pre-pare for the day when they may be forced to respond to an act of terrorism.

Faced with a new form of civic violence, the academic com-munity has responded with a series of books, monographs, and articles in what is rapidly becoming a new field of specialization in the behavioral sciences. Terrorism is now a leading topic for academic inquiry.

Yet, despite this genuine concern, the response of all parties is often fragmented. The specialists in the different professions and disciplines often tend to go it along and approach the "problem" of terrorism from their different perspectives. While domestic, transnational, and international terrorists increasingly engage in concerted and systematic attacks on the world order, there is a paucity of integrated programs in which specialists can integrate their different skills to respond effectively to the alliances formed by the new terrorists.

This book integrates the concerns and skills of the operationally oriented representatives of law-enforcement agencies with social-science techniques in order to assist the policy makers at all levels who are ultimately responsible for dealing with acts of terrorism. It presents a detailed analysis of a simulation technique developed to provide the most realistic training possible for those who must respond to hostage-taking in general and those who one day may have to deal with the additional complexities surrounding a politically motivated terrorist seizure. Simulation is a dynamic approach that not only provides vital training but also can be used to evaluate fully the forces designated to deal with a threat. Programs that emphasize procedural checklists often break down under the stress of actual events. Simulation avoids that danger. At the same time it provides a means by which police and policy makers can test existing plans, revise them, or develop new measures based on training that generates the pressures that occur in actual incidents. The detailed analyses of simulations in this book raise a series of questions that should be considered by the officials and organizations who must prepare to deal with the complex and shifting characteristics of contemporary terrorism.

2 Just Another Incident

On June 24 five people met at a house near a large southwestern state university. The group, four men and one woman, came from different backgrounds but shared a common purpose—to succeed in seizing and holding hostages at a regional airport. The leader of the group, John, was a highly trained Vietnam veteran. He would use the skills he acquired as a member of the Special Forces against the civilian and military elite, whom he detested. Alienated from the college kids who drank in the bar he ran, John was now going to get his revenge against those who had ignored his service on the front lines in the war.

Michael, John's drinking buddy, fought another kind of war in the seminars at the university. A brilliant ideologue, he rejected the phony paper commitment of those who only wrote about the need for revolutionary action. He was now dedicated to a plan to strike back at the parasites in the industrial order.

Robert, the least articulate individual in the group, was a follower. He admired John and wanted only to be like him. A dropout, he had little direction in his life and joined causes to make friends.

Perhaps the most intelligent and sensitive was Roberta. A doctoral candidate in English, she had been part of the action in Berkeley and had worked with the Weathermen and other radical groups. She had come home to the town where she was reared. She despised it for its parochialism, but it was vulnerable to an assault to make the pigs realize that there was no safe haven in a people's war.

Don was the fifth member of the group. A carpenter by profession, he was always on the edge of a rage, a rage that he could neither understand nor control. He would follow Roberta anywhere.

In the previous two weeks the members of the group had skillfully evaluated potential targets. Drawing on their knowledge of the city, they were well acquainted with the area in which they would operate. Furthermore, all of them had friends who would offer them indirect support if the need arose. As in a military operation, the band had effectively carried out the intelligence function. John was particularly adept in obtaining information about the state of readiness of the local police force. He was aided by military experience and his ownership of the bar, which gave him a splendid locale in which to keep up with the local gossip.

The group decided to seize hostages at the terminal of the regional airport located fifteen miles outside town. Because the airport had never been subjected to such an attack, the group correctly assessed that the local police were relatively complacent. There was every reason to believe that a well-executed assault would accomplish the mission.

Michael was particularly pleased that the assault would be launched against randomly selected hostages. He felt that such a tactic would force an often-indifferent public to recognize that in the new people's war there were no such things as asylum or innocent people. Roberta, for her part, recognized that the seizure of hostages at a modern airport would help dramatize the attack and bring the media running to the scene. Certainly the coverage would be far more extensive than if they took a more conventional route and robbed a bank in the tradition of Carlos Marighella, who refined the techniques of "armed propaganda" in his struggle against Latin-American reactionaries.[1]

The acquisition of weapons was relatively easy. John was able to obtain M-16s from friends who had acquired them during their days in the service. All the weapons were quickly reconverted to fire on automatic. Other rifles and pistols were obtained without difficulty. The group bought the rifles from gun collectors and purchased pistols from a large discount store.

The group stole dynamite from a construction site. To refine their arsenal further, Roberta visited a local army-navy store, where she picked up training grenades. When asked what she needed them for, Roberta said they were to be props in a little-theater production. They looked real and would make the terrorist threat even more credible.

After the acquisition of the weapons, the group prepared a final plan for the attack, which was to take place on July 7.

The local chief of police had his own concerns. A bond issue was shortly to be voted on, and there was hope that a new headquarters building would be funded if the issue passed. While he had read about potential threats of terrorism in the *Police Chief* and had received updated information on dissident groups, his jurisdiction had never been subjected to a politically motivated hostage-taking. To be sure, his officers had been in barricaded situations when criminals were caught in the act, but fortunately the perpetrators had surrendered.

Lieutenant White was a real hot wire in the department. As head of the newly established tactical unit he had conducted a few weekend exercises with the team. All the members of the unit looked forward to the competition with the tactical unit in the next city. The contests were a welcome relief from the daily routine. White was sure that his unit would develop into a fine organization. After all, it contained some of the best marksmen in the county.

Sergeant Williams had recently undergone negotiation training in a short course taught by an FBI agent in the city. He had been annoyed that he was temporarily detached from his supervisory position on the late-night shift—he enjoyed his newly awarded rank. He had reasoned, however, that the course gave him one more certification that would help him on the lieutenant's examination. He had been joined in the course by Scotty, a very senior patrol officer, who seemed happy to stay on his beat until retirement.

On the morning of July 7 the air terminal was relatively quiet. An early flight was scheduled for Dallas, and five passengers were waiting to go to the boarding gate. One passenger, Lieutenant Colonel Marks, was particularly concerned that the plane would leave on time. He was scheduled to assume a new position as personnel officer at a large air base. He met his old friend Jim Berger, who was also scheduled to take the flight. Jim worked for a large multinational corporation in Latin America and had just completed home leave. The other passengers were an elderly couple and a college student who was going home after a short intersession course.

At 8:00 A.M., Patrol Officer Rodgers was looking forward to the end of a long shift. He did not like the monotony of the airport security duty, but it was a welcome change from his old beat, which had inflamed his ulcer. The police surgeon agreed that the new duty would be good for him. Rodgers idly chatted with the private guard who was adjusting the X-ray machine. It had been on the blink.

By 8:30 all the passengers were heading down the sanitized corridor to board the plane. Five late arrivals joined them. They appeared to be a group of college students from the local university. They were carrying a lot of hand luggage.

At 8:36 the attack began. John quickly opened his case and took out the stockless M-16. The other members of the group followed suit. Patrol Officer Rodgers did not believe what was happening and was quickly disarmed. The passengers and the security guard were shocked and listened numbly to the abuse heaped on them by Don. They were all searched, bound, and led to an empty observation tower by the boarding area, where for ten cents visitors could have a commanding view of the airport and listen to the conversations between the traffic controllers and the pilots.

As the terrorists began putting paper over the windows and securing the doors, a local airline representative, who had seen the takeover from his position, recovered his composure and called the police department. The desk sergeant initially thought that it was a crank call. After all, who would have believed that an armed band would seize hostages here? That was something that would happen in Germany or Italy. But the dispatcher notified a patrol unit to check out the scene. Thirty minutes later the patrol reported that the windows of the observation deck were almost entirely covered, that they could dimly see an armed and hooded man, and that a series of demands had been posted outside the door leading to the deck.

Confronted with the incident, the watch commander called the chief, who immediately came to the station. The chief called in all available personnel to establish a perimeter at the airport and notified Lieutenant White that the tactical unit should be activated. The chief also alerted the FBI and the state police.

At 10:05 A.M. a written list of demands was brought to the command center, which had been established in the airport manager's office. The demands were accompanied by a threat that unless a million dollars and an aircraft were delivered to the group—which called itself the New World Revolutionary Movement—the hostages would be killed. Confronted with the threat, the chief called in his negotiators. But there was a problem: there were no telephones in the observation tower with which to communicate with the terrorists.

The chief initially asked the local field commander to attempt to use a bullhorn. Unfortunately there was a strong wind, and his voice would not carry to the observation tower, much less penetrate its walls. An attempt was then made to employ a field telephone, but it malfunctioned. Its batteries had not been checked in over two years. Communications were finally established when the local telephone company representative cut through red tape and provided the necessary equipment for the police. Delay could have been avoided if a procedure had been developed for such a situation.

Finally, two hours after the initial seizure, negotiations began. Because of the delay, the hostages had begun to assume that nothing was being done to secure their release. Isolated from the frantic activities that were taking place, they could not know that a concerted response strategy was very slowly being developed. The terrorists, for their part, were angered at the delay, and Don lost his temper at times. Still, the group had come prepared for a long siege. They were eating in front of the frightened, but increasingly hungry victims.

By this time the crisis, or command, center was in full operation. Although a routine had been established, the inherent strains of dealing with the siege were intensified because of jurisdictional disputes and a personality conflict between the chief and the special agent in charge of the local FBI office. The chief felt that the hostage-takers, despite their demands, were nothing more than common criminals who fell under the jurisdiction of his department. The special agent contended that the armed group had clearly proved that they were engaged in an act of political terrorism, a potential skyjacking, which placed the responsibility with the Bureau. Because of this debate, effective coordination among the responding forces was limited. Moreover, the debate took place in full view of members of the media, who had persuaded a newly assigned police press officer to let them into the crisis center.

Sergeant Williams conducted the initial negotiations while Patrol Officer Scotty acted as log taker. The chief was tempted to negotiate directly but knew that it would be unwise for him to talk with the terrorists. Furthermore, he had his hands full trying to coordinate the responding units. For one thing, the radios were on different frequencies, and it would take time before a command net was established.

Despite his training, Williams quickly realized that he was ill prepared to negotiate. The noise level in the command post, the conflicting advice, and the gravity of the situation made it difficult for him to employ the methods he had learned in his short course. Moreover, he was not used to listening to criminals: as a sergeant he was used to giving commands. Consequently he did not establish any rapport with the hostages and, worse yet, angered Michael, the spokesman for the group, by calling him a wise-ass college kid. Scotty took over after the terrorists refused to speak with Williams, but the initial damage had been done.

In the ensuing hours Patrol Officer Scotty intuitively drew on his experience in the field and his ability to listen, a skill he had refined in the countless domestic disputes he had had to resolve over the years. A grudging relationship of minimal trust was developing between him and Michael, and a routine was being established. Yet both the chief and Scotty refused to send food to the hostages unless they received something in return. Michael refused to release a hostage as a sign of good faith, and he told Scotty that it was up to the police to prove their good intentions. The result was a deadlock.

As evening came, tension and fatigue began to grip the antagonists on both sides of the barricade. The negotiation process did speed up as a result of a medical emergency, in which one hostage—an elderly man—was released in exchange for food, but there were no other breakthroughs.

At 9:00 P.M. a shot was heard on the observation deck, and shortly thereafter a body was thrown on the Tarmac. Confronted with this act, the chief chose to use the tactical option. Under the command of Lieutenant White the tactical team launched an assault. In the ensuing fight three of the hostages were killed, and the remaining two were seriously injured. Three of the terrorists were also fatally shot, and one was wounded. Lieutenant White was killed. Michael escaped in the confusion.

For the surviving hostages the scars remain. The multinational-corporation executive will no longer travel in disturbed areas. The lieutenant colonel has learned that his prisoner-of-war training did not equip him to cope successfully with the experience of being a hostage.

The story, which received extensive national coverage, was shortly overshadowed by another attack involving the seizure of an aircraft in West Germany.

3 Definition Is a Question of Life or Death, Not a Semantic Exercise

To the surviving victims of terrorism the physical and emotional scars are an irrefutable and personal horror. To the families and friends of those who do not survive the memories of the act are an immutable legacy. The carnage and bloodshed are objective acts experienced or witnessed. Terrorism needs no definition for those who are directly or indirectly its victims.

To those who observe the act, to those who must respond to it, and to the policy makers and academics who are concerned with analyzing and devising programs to meet the threat, contemporary terrorism is an act of violence that cannot be simply defined. Often it is a subjective phenomenon open to interpretation even while the victims await their uncertain fates. The subjective responses to terrorism create different meanings for those who are forced to accept its presence. The police may interpret an act of terrorism as simply another form of criminal violence. While such an interpretation can provide order in the chaos, it may also limit the ability of the responding forces to develop a choice of effective strategies to meet the threat after a terrorist act has taken place. There is a difference between those who terrorize while engaging in a crime and those who systematically use terror as a political weapon to achieve political goals. If authorities do not face the subjective aspects of terrorist incidents, they may not only seal the fate of the victims but also lend an air of legitimacy and dignity to the very people they are trying to apprehend. If the police, for example, overreact and bring massive force to bear on what is essentially a criminal act, they may give credibility to the perpetrators on the other side of the barricade.

While it is generally recognized that political terrorists know how to achieve their goals by dramatic acts, the responding forces often do not know that their own actions may define the roles of those whom they are facing. Confronted with the subjective reality of the act, the police, nevertheless, must respond. It is no simple task. In their strategy and tactics the responding forces face the complex challenge of dealing with ambiguity. In selecting the weapons to be employed or the negotiating position to be taken, the law-enforcement community must develop flexible responses even though there is an equally important requirement for discipline and direction. The subjective dimensions of terroristic violence must be recognized. To define the response simply in terms of the police versus the criminals is to ignore the different motivations and training of criminals and political terrorists. Difficult decisions must be made that call for concerted action. Those who act must recognize that there is an ambiguity that cannot be eliminated by simple tactical solutions.

The policy makers must also recognize the subjectivity that surrounds acts of terrorism. On the one hand, the policy maker must not fall into the trap of defining terrorism with such relativism that it becomes all but impossible to fashion a coherent response strategy. The often-obtuse debates within the United Nations over what constitutes terrorism are perfect examples. Under the old saw "One man's terrorist in another man's liberator," relativism can immobilize attempts to respond to the real threat and also can be an excuse for inaction or, worse yet, a justification for further acts of violence.[1] On the other hand, the policy makers must avoid the opposite extreme of attempting artificially to impose administrative certainty on the ambiguity that surrounds acts of terrorism. To characterize all forms of terrorism simply as forms of criminality may lead to idealistic, simplistic solutions where the so-called resolution of the problem is little more than moralizing by authorities against the wrong-doers. If there is to be "war on terrorism," it must take place on many fronts, in many ways, and cannot be conducted simply by administrative fiat.

The vexing questions concerning the subjective aspects of terrorism also confront the academic profession. Exhaustive amounts of time have been devoted to the complexities involved in defining terrorism. Elaborate classification systems have been devised, and the ethical questions related to terrorism are constantly being addressed. There is a danger that such exercises may at times degenerate into an intellectual game in which the concern over theories and abstractions has little relationship to the violent acts that we have witnessed. Yet it must be recognized that the quest for definitions is more than a semantic battle. Unless there is common agreement on the definition and characteristics of terrorism, there can be no development of systematic research and analysis of particular types of violence. If the term *terror* is defined too generally, the scope of the analysis may be too broad, and the findings may be meaningless. If the definition is too narrow, there is little opportunity for comparative analysis, which can show patterns common to a variety of acts of terrorism. The common patterns must be understood if there is to be a choice of effective responses.

A sophisticated terrorist aptly uses the objective factors and the subjective ambiguities that surround the terroristic act both to justify violence and to confound those who must meet the threat. The systematic and skillful use of terror tactics is often cleverly orchestrated to produce fear in the intended victims and in those who are watching. The finality of an act of carnage gives the terrorist the credibility to be viewed as a real threat. He often justifies the action by the absolute righteousness of the cause. Yet, even as he is establishing the credibility of the threat by an act of violence and justifying it as a historical necessity or a moral imperative, the skillful practitioner of terroristic violence also confounds and immobilizes those who must respond to the deed by attempting to be many things to many people.

Through the act of violence the terrorist may project the image of a modern Robin Hood to some, a patriot to others, and a vicious killer to still others. In such a way he may gain the support of the romantic in the first instance, the idealist in the second, and force authority to overreact in the third. Thus he establishes a state of siege. Terrorists are often fanatics, but it must be recognized that they may play skillfully on ambiguity to set one party against another and effectively block attempts to develop unified and coherent policies.

Those who directly experience an act of terrorism should be concerned with subjective factors in the face of the threat to their lives, but in the long term they too may face the problem of coping with ambiguity. A group of passengers on a skyjacked plane, a government official confined to a "people's prison," and a kidnapped multinational–corporation executive must understand the motivation, the tactics, and the strategies of their captors if they are not passively going to accept their fate as victims. It makes a difference if the hostage can recognize the difference between the behavior patterns of a criminal caught in the act and a political terrorist who intentionally seizes hostages as a means of dramatizing a cause, making political demands, or obtaining funds for the continuing revolutionary battle.

Acts of Terrorism Are Not Happenings:
They Are Violence with a Purpose

Despite the ambiguity and subjectivity that may surround an act of terrorism, there are certain characteristics that differentiate terrorism from other violent criminal acts. While the indiscriminate murders, maimings, and mayhem associated with terrorism often appear to result from irrational behavior by the terrorist, it is important to assume that the violence, however barbaric, has its own rationality. This point may be difficult to accept, but unless the responding forces and concerned officials do so, they will not be able to differentiate between terroristic violence and other forms of strife and will fail to understand the patterns that take place when the hostage-taker initiates an incident. Acts of terrorism are not to be treated as just another form of criminal violence.

Unlike the criminal who may see fear as incidental to the crime, the terrorist intentionally and systematically employs terror as a weapon to achieve his objectives. The resort to terror is instrumental and purposeful. The terrorist's act often appears irrational to the victims and observers, but to the terrorist it has meaning and direction. While we find it reprehensible, it is justified to its practitioner, and its meaning to him must be appreciated if an effective response strategy is to be established. Even if the terrorist is clearly mentally disturbed and appears to practice terror for its own sake, the authorities must look for the motivation and purpose behind what appears to be the work of an unthinking fanatic or deranged individual. It is essential that those who counter the threat understand the perception of those who are engaging in the act of terrorism. In some instances the motivation and goals will be easy to discern, in others they may be difficult to see, but it is crucial that there be a quest for understanding of the dynamics behind the act. The importance of the quest for explanations—often under great pressure—cannot be overstated. Unless the responding forces and, indeed, the victims begin to discern reasons for and patterns in the actions of the terrorists, they may be immobilized in the face of what appears to be an act of deliberate chaos.

Briefly defined, terrorism is the systematic threat or use of force to achieve certain goals. Unlike most other criminals, the terrorist employs violence or the threat of violence to instill fear not only in the victims but also in a broader audience. The terrorist act may actually be aimed at "the people watching."[2] This instilling of fear or, in a more intense state, a sense of overwhelming dread, is meant to change the attitudes not only of the victims but also of the responding forces and an even larger audience. The psychological ingredients of modern-day terrorism may in the long run be more significant than the actual physical acts. Terrorists attempt to make victims of us all even though individual targets are selected. It is the unstated sense of dread, the fear of the unknown, that breaks down our indifference and forces us to recognize that we may be just as vulnerable as the immediate victims. The skillful terrorist plays on the vulnerability of a larger target group beyond those caught on the other side of the barricade. The members of the Red Brigades and the Baader-Meinhof gang have breached the detachment and indifference of a general public. By their actions they have presented a threat that is salient to our experiences: we too are vulnerable. Often the private recognition of this vulnerability makes a single act of terror ten thousand miles away from the TV viewer's home far more fearsome personally than the carnage associated with conventional war. We cannot find security in the role of noncombatants removed from the field of battle. By their acts the terrorists instill a fear that in the long term is pernicious to a broad set of potential victims beyond the immediate targets of the physical acts of terroristic violence.

This ability to force a wider audience to accept their vulnerability is in part related to two technological innovations that are only a few decades old. The introduction of jet aircraft in the late 1950s gave the modern terrorist the physical capacity to select targets of opportunity globally. The terrorist can declare a war against all because there are no longer any safe havens based on political and physical boundaries. Television and satellite communication also enable the terrorist to break through the insularity of the larger audience. They spread a message of fear and intimidation worldwide almost instantaneously. Terrorism is now a systematic assault against the international order.

Although a mass audience is at times indirectly victimized by terrorist violence, it is to the potential immediate victims that this book is directed. By understanding the rationality in the outwardly irrational acts of violence, by accepting that one may be a victim personally, the immediate targets of terrorism need not simply ignore or accept their fate blindly. For those who may experience terror, the global threat can and must be understood from a much shorter perspective—the confines of an aircraft cabin, a people's prison, or the street outside a pub in Londonderry when a bomb is exploded.

Political Terrorism is in the Eye of the Beholder

The line between criminal violence and terrorism is often obscure or unrecognized, and the understanding of the essentially new kind of conflict is further hampered by the issues associated with political terrorism. Often a circular logic is employed in addressing the question. It is not uncommon for definitions to state that political terrorism is either terror employed for political purposes or terror having political impact. Such a definition, of course, lacks precision. It aptly illustrates again the ambiguity that surrounds the terroristic act, which is outwardly a concrete act of violence of a particular kind.

There are certainly clear instances of political terrorism. The justification for the Munich massacre by the Palestine Liberation Organization (PLO), the Israeli assassination of PLO leaders in response, the bombings by the Armed Forces of National Liberation for Puerto Rico (FALN) in New York apparently fit nearly in the category. But, while the motivation and justification for the acts may be stated in political rhetoric, in many instances political terms are appended to incidents of terrorism that are not clearly politically motivated. Car bombings in Ulster may be justified in terms of political objectives, but to the bombers and their accomplices the acts may at times be little more than sectarian assassinations.[3] To the individual members of the Red Brigades political terrorism may be primarily a justification for violent behavior that may not be motivated by politics. Will the motivations of the new generation of international terrorists be based on political conviction or on the desire to follow the paths of the soldiers of fortune and mercenaries who preceded them?

The gray area is further obscured by the behavior of observers and of those who respond to the acts of violence and by the terrorists' manipulation of the observers' perceptions. An act that at its inception was clearly criminal can by degrees take on political overtones and can later become political because of such diverse factors as the status of the victims, the behavior of the hostage-taker, the response of the police, the coverage of the media, and so on. In the Hanafi siege, when Islamic ambassadors acted as negotiators, a criminal act became an international affair as the representative of sovereign powers sat down with the representatives of an obscure sect. As one senior British law-enforcement official noted in telling how an administrative response can define an act, "The act is political when the Foreign Office calls my office."[4] Just as criminals by their actions can wear "political garments" and thus take on an air of importance and, indeed, legitimacy, so can the responding police, corporations, and media covering the event convert what is apolitical into a political cause célèbre. Those who deal with the terrorist threat must have the sensitivity and foresight not to be trapped into playing into the hands of the criminal politically; they must recognize that by their actions they in part define the nature of the action. Accommodating and operationalizing ambiguity is more than a semantic battle. It is a question of life or death. Definitions determine tactical and strategic responses.

4 Acts of Terrorism, or the Theater of the Obscene

The terroristic violence that we witness on television often becomes a grim play in which the terrorists, the victims, and a broader audience both consciously and unconsciously play out their respective roles. In this form of theater the individual acts appear to be characterized by high drama and uncertainty, but the total terrorist scenario often takes on a level of predictability that desensitizes those who watch the various incidents unfold. The audience may be gripped temporarily by the events they witness or, concomitantly, may lose interest if the events are merely repetitious, reported incorrectly, or not reported at all. The level of drama of the obscene play depends upon a number of factors, including the setting, the actors, the media, and the audience.

The setting where the terrorist act takes place may largely determine the degree of impact and the size of the audience. If the bombing or hostage-taking occurs in an isolated rural setting—no matter how significant the victims—the audience will probably be limited because of a lack of media coverage and a feeling that the violence is geographically and mentally peripheral to the audience's concern. But if the setting is urban, the drama inherent in a mass setting may result in media coverage that will have far more impact than the most barbaric act in a rural confine. The murder of a village official in a hamlet during an ongoing insurgency may create great trauma among a limited audience, including those personally acquainted with the victim, but it hardly produces the broad involvement that results when the victims act out their roles to a mass audience in a mass society. If the whole world is to watch, the event probably will not take place in a backwater setting. Contemporary terrorism, which is largely the product of a communications revolution, is primarily an urban event, unlike the terrorism associated with rural insurgencies. Even the development of urban guerrilla warfare partly depends on getting the event across to the largest audience in the shortest possible time.

If the setting is not urban and cosmopolitan, the drama can still have great impact if it is played out in an inherently exciting or unique setting. That is why a skyjacking by a lone, deranged gunman may have more meaning than the murder of a large group in a pub in Ulster. When the plane seeks permission to land, the skyjacking instantaneously becomes an international affair as the plane crosses border after border and the event is reported by the wire services. When the plane lands, the inherent drama continues. The grim odyssey of mankind's technological genius is a far more stirring spectacle than a conventional act of violence in a rural hamlet or, for that matter, on a city street. The impact may be magnified in the future when terrorists seek out other sophisticated and significant high-technology targets, such as nuclear facilities and refineries.

The impact is determined not only by the setting but also by the type of act. As a consequence setting and action are often closely interrelated. Bombings, for example, do not have the dramatic power of an ongoing hostage-taking unless they are coordinated and directed against a highly visible targets or they are particularly bloody. While the shock of seeing the bodies of the dead or wounded may penetrate our indifference, the act is essentially over for the audience. The ambulances take the victims to the hospital or to the morgue, and only the friends and relatives are left to grieve. But when the fate of the victims is still to be determined, the play goes on, the finale has not been written, the uncertainty and suspense remain. The audience will watch unless the act goes on too long. A siege of a day may be inherently more successful with the media audience than a pro-tracted hostage-taking where the kidnapped victim cannot be seen unless the victim has major symbolic value as Patty Hearst did. Ominously, we have been increasingly able to witness the agony of the hostage. Terrorism by videotape has already taken place, as when Hans Martin Schleyer, a West German business-man, made his appeal from an underground prison that was turned into a filming studio.

As in the case of other plays, the dramatic impact will, of course, be judged on the quality of the individual actors and how they interact. If the victim is not seen by the audience, if his appeal cannot be heard, if his terror cannot be shared, he may be nothing more than a phantom to the audience—a phan-tom to be pitied but hardly related to—but, if we can see the terror in the faces of the victims, the event will play on the mor-bid curiosity that impels people to go to the site of an accident. As for the terrorists, they must either intentionally or uncon-sciously establish their dramatic credibility. While a terrorist dressed in civilian clothes and holding a small automatic weap-on is just as much a threat as a terrorist wearing a mask, dressed in a military uniform, and brandishing the same weapon, the images of fear are portrayed more effectively in the latter case. For example, in February, 1977, a disgruntled and mentally un-balanced man in Indianapolis, holding a shotgun by a wire noose to a mortgage-company executive's head and shouting obscenities, was infinitely more compelling than any profes-sional assassin coolly pointing a rifle at a potential victim's heart and saying nothing.

The responding forces by their very acts intensify or reduce the dramatic thrust of the event. Police officers in body armor with special weapons, tactics teams taking their positions, bull-horns, and high-powered floodlights are certainly more dra-matic than a low-profile siege where the weapons are deployed but not seen.

Press coverage may determine not only whether there is an

audience for an event but also whether they find it appealing. After all, hostage-taking can become a protracted and therefore tedious occurrence unless there are interviews with distraught relatives and victims, or, better yet, the terrorists. If the terrorists devise their own form of guerrilla theater and conduct press conferences in a building in Washington, D.C., or on a runway at a deserted airfield in the desert, they not only make their cause known but also make it dramatically appealing—a story to be covered.

In the long run, of course, the impact of the event will be determined by how all the parties interact. If the terrorist's threat is viewed as credible or at least novel, if the victims are properly visible and terrified, if the responding authorities bring their force to bear, and if the media cover the event, it will be a good drama for the audience. Unfortunately, it will be a drama with potentially disastrous results for both the witting and the unwitting actors.

Recognizing and Countering the Theatrical Aspects of Terrorism

Given the inherent drama and theatricality of contemporary terrorism, it seems logical to employ elements of the performing arts, in conjunction with social-science methods and operational tactics drawn from the law-enforcement and military professions, to develop training programs to counter the continuing threat. While the bomb-maker or hostage-taker may not recognize that he is participating in a grim play, and while the responding forces may find it difficult to perceive themselves as actors on a unique stage, a recognition of the dramatic factor is important if the terrorists are to be denied the opportunity to play to a global audience. Moreover, the recognition of the "theater of the obscene" is increasingly important with the emergence of terrorists who are schooled in the techniques of media coverage and media manipulation.

The development of training programs to meet the terrorist threat may be flawed if theatrical techniques are ignored. In actual incidents the participants either intuitively or intentionally play roles, however ill-defined. Although the dynamics and conclusions of the incidents are not formally scripted, and the outcomes consequently are fraught with uncertainty, there are still elements in an actual crisis that parallel a theatrical performance. There is a scenario, particularly among the dedicated professional terrorists, in the form of their plan of action. The plan is the basis for a script that determines the life or death of all the participants. The motivation behind the terrorist act defines the role played by the initiators of the drama. The list of demands is drawn up, the goals are declared, the target or setting is decided, and the victims or protagonists are selected. The victims assume their roles unwillingly, but they too, intuitively or intentionally, assist in playing out the drama. There is an expectation on the part of the terrorist about how the other parties will react. Often there is a conscious attempt to create an incident that will provoke a reaction from the responding forces and the media and make the event intensely interesting to the widest audience possible. Finally, those responding to the incident may have unintentionally rehearsed their responses in contingency plans and training, which ensure a degree of predictability in the midst of crisis. The special-weapons and tactics team establishes an inner and outer perimeter, the command post is established, and the hostage negotiators prepare to assume their role while the media watches. The play begins. Even if the script is not formalized and the outcome is uncertain, the theatrical elements still intrude throughout the duration of an incident. Terrorism has the attributes of improvisational theater: the ultimate plot and the conclusion of the drama are determined by how the performers interact in the environment where they have been placed. There is, however, one major difference between improvisational theater and terrorism: there is no director to guide the drama and provide the ultimate tone. The direction and outcome are not monopolized by any single person or group. The drama is the product of the interaction among all the participants, who through their actions determine how the play will be resolved.

Confronted with the terrorist theater of the obscene, the authorities have at times ignored the dramatic elements of terrorist incidents in developing training programs to meet the threat. The programs consequently often are flawed from their inception, and the training may ultimately fail to prepare units to develop an effective response. Worse yet, the programs may instill a false sense of preparedness, which can be worse than no specialized training at all.

The responses of the law-enforcement community and the military have often ignored not only the theatrical aspects of terrorism but also the complex interpersonal dynamics that are a part of even the most "simplest" incident. All too often emphasis has been placed on doing things by the numbers. This stress on procedures and mechanistic responses often produces only formalistic responses to the complex behavioral factors in an incident, but it is understandable because of the emphasis placed on orderly and predictable procedures in military and quasi-military organizations. There are undoubtedly valid reasons for rigorous discipline and control in developing tactical responses. Still, the resulting response may lack the flexibility and sensitivity essential to deal with the uncertainty that characterizes individual and collective behavior under great stress during an actual incident. Too much emphasis on routine in training for a potential crisis ignores the lack of predictability and the disorder that occur when the terrorists take central stage. Formalism may prepare the responding personnel to counter a complex incident with only an empty series of procedures, which break down under pressure.

This emphasis on procedural responses intensifies further from the operational units. When middle- and upper-level policy makers are being prepared for incidents, the choices are no longer even viewed as procedural in content. At a higher level the choices run the danger of being converted into a series of bureaucratic responses very far removed from the dynamics and complexities of an actual incident. The bureaucratic rationale offers a sense that an effective strategy is being prepared to meet a threat, but the strategy may stem from a false image of predictability and be ineffective in the press of actual events. Furthermore, while the responding field units do receive training—however flawed—the middle-level and senior policy makers are rarely given realistic and continuous preparation until they face on-the-job training in the midst of an actual incident. Such techniques as "crisis management" are emphasized at all levels of bureaucracy, but the techniques need to be tested in a realistic setting.

The fashioning of effective training programs is further complicated by the manner in which the programs are devised and evaluated. Until recently many programs and exercises were developed for the law-enforcement community or the military by other members of the respective profession. Since it is the mission of those forces to meet the terrorist threat it appeared logical that they should train their own personnel. Since the military and quasimilitary organizations respond bureaucratically to incidents of terrorism, that bias will enter into whatever training programs they devise. Even more disconcerting is the narrow perspective shared by those who devise and receive the training: as members of the same profession they speak the same language. Precisely because of this they run the risk of not developing effective programs to meet the threat situation. Although the police and military units and the officials in charge of countering the threat share common values and orientations, those values and orientations are not shared by the terrorists, who are outsiders and enemies of the civil order and as such devise their own techniques to wage an undeclared war. Thus, while civil agencies provide training to meet "the clandestine threat,"[1] the training is often based on the authorities' perception of terrorist tactics and strategies, a perception that may be only distantly related to how terrorists actually conduct their missions. When training takes place—however well motivated and executed—there is the danger of a false understanding of terrorist tactics and strategies. Law-enforcement personnel often play the terrorist roles, and the responding parties may execute their mission effectively in training sessions because their opponents are still working on the same assumptions and procedures. It is simply not enough to look and talk like the law-enforcement and military perception of a terrorist. For the policeman-terrorist to be effective, he must think like one. He must get into his role.

When the participants in the training all come from the same organizations and professions, the evaluation of the exercises runs the risk of becoming a matter of mutual reinforcement. There may be an understandable, but dangerous, unwillingness to submit to external evaluation by individuals who—like the terrorist—are not a part of the law-enforcement community. If the training is to be realistically conceived, executed, and evaluated, it must be realistic theater—theater in which people get into their roles, theater in which the roles are not muted and artificial because the actors have played them before and have studied under the same teachers.

The Study Group on International Terrorism

Because of the problems in training programs, a new approach to hostage negotiations and antiterrorist operations was developed by the Study Group on International Terrorism at the University of Oklahoma. Composed primarily of graduate students with the assistance of faculty and off-campus personnel, this essentially ad hoc group of individuals systematically began to analyze incidents of terrorism worldwide. In early studies and in a continuing analysis of available data certain patterns became evident that were common to many incidents of hostage-taking related to political terrorism. In addition, serious questions of policy on the local, national, and international level surfaced in the studies. As a result of the preliminary findings the Study Group decided to employ their analysis of terrorist incidents in devising simulations for military and police units. The simulation technique afforded a means by which the systematic analysis of information could be used in training exercises that recognized the theatrical aspects of political terrorism.

Over ten exercises have been conducted in the Study Group's series of simulations, including a pioneering exercise under very controlled conditions with the University of Oklahoma Police Department and a more detailed exercise that was part of a seminar for public officials at the state, local, and national level at the university airfield with units of the Norman Police Department. In addition to those home-based programs a wide variety of other simulations were conducted. A highly realistic, tactically sophisticated simulation took place at a deserted airfield in the Panama Canal Zone with the Seventh Special Forces Group (Airborne). It partially addressed the question of how effectively a military force could respond to a hostage-taking incident. The international elements in a terrorist threat were subject to further evaluation when I conducted a simulation with units of the New Zealand Police as part of a hostage negotiation course. Two additional overseas exercises were held with personnel from the 51st Security Police Squadron, Osan Air Force Base, Korea. Another military-associated exercise was developed with the Minot, North Dakota, Police Department, a North Dakota Special Weapons and Tactics Team, and members of a seminar on international terrorism that included personnel from the 91st Security Squadron at Minot Air Force Base.

Two other complex simulations were conducted. One was held in conjunction with a seminar sponsored by the Port of Portland Police Department at the Portland, Oregon, International Airport. Participants included the Multnomah County Division of Public Safety, the Gresham Police Department, the Troutdale Police Department, air police from the Oregon Air National Guard, and representatives from the city of Portland and other agencies. The other simulation involved the seizure of a facility at the Sun Oil Refinery in downtown Tulsa, Oklahoma, in order to evaluate the response of the Special Operations Team of the Tulsa Police Department.

In addition to the simulations three other kinds of programs were conducted. The first of these was primarily a classroom exercise under the direction of faculty members at the National

War College for an elected course entitled, "New Forms of Violence."[2] The program was particularly concerned with developing effective crisis-management techniques at the national level for an incident of international terrorism. In conjunction with all those programs, a highly specialized staged exercise was developed for a leading international airline, which has now integrated the simulation into the security training of their flight attendants.[3]

A number of the exercises were filmed on videotape for presentation and analysis.[4] In addition, logs and observations by the participants were collected. Finally, in a number of simulations open-ended questionnaires were distributed to the participants for analysis later.

There was a wide variety of unique elements in all of the exercises, but certain common patterns emerged in the behavior of those involved in terrorist incidents including seizure of hostages. The patterns can assist authorities to develop more effective training programs in preparation for potential incidents. While the findings do not represent a final analysis of the information drawn from all of the simulations, they are a substantial basis for continuing research into training techniques and into responses to the terrorist threat.

5 Writing the Terrorist Plot

The development of a simulation combines the analysis and application of terrorist tactics and strategies with an exercise in imagination. In the formulation and execution of the exercises—from the development of the plot (the scenario) to the writing of the script (the operations order), the actual performance (the simulation), and the subsequent reviews (the evaluation)—a mixture of approaches utilizes different disciplines and professions to evolve the most realistic and challenging program possible. The methodology of the social sciences provides the comparative analysis of incidents on which the scenario is based. Military tactics and strategies are constantly refined to develop as credible and challenging a threat as possible for the responding forces. The theatrical arts are employed not only to reproduce the "theater of the obscene" but also to intensify the emotions and consequent tensions to the level of actual incidents. In procedural exercises in the military and law-enforcement community individuals may never fully get into their roles, but a simulation forces the participants to play their respective roles with a degree of commitment and identification that obscures the fact that the exercise is only an imitation of reality. The line between the terrorist "play" and the terrorist act is deliberately blurred in a successful exercise. The emotions and subjective responses that are released once an assault is initiated test more than the tactical skills of the participants and their equipment. The simulation forces the participants to assume the roles that they may have to undertake in real life. They may go on a voyage to self-discovery by seeing and experiencing how they react, individually and collectively, under stress.

Establishing the Scenario

The initial stage in preparing for a simulation is the development of the scenario for the operations order and the terrorist attack. Seven elements go into the writing of the scenario:

1. An ongoing, comparative analysis of past and present incidents, building into the simulation common tactical and strategic patterns.

2. A study of tactics, weapons, targets, and other technical factors that may influence future trends in terrorist operations.

3. An assessment of potential threats within the jurisdictions where the exercise will be conducted. This assessment integrates a projection of potential incidents with an evaluation of the intelligence officers who are members of the responding units.

4. Customizing the scenario so that the particular training of the participating units can be evaluated under the most realistic conditions possible.

5. Modification of the scenario so that the simulators can examine different patterns of behavior as part of a continuing research agenda.

6. Refinement of the scenario to reflect the ideological concerns and personalities of the individuals who will assume the roles of the terrorists, their levels of tactical sophistication, and their previous training.

7. Additional inputs unknown to the terrorists that are developed by the simulation director in order to build into the exercise more uncertainty, tension, and realism.

Building the Scenario: A Data Construct

In the construction of the scenario for a simulation, emphasis is placed on incorporating into the planned assault the comparative analysis of past incidents. In this manner the scenario, the subsequent operations order, and the resulting simulation contain patterns of action and response that are present in actual terrorist incidents. The details of the tactical and strategic measures utilized in actual simulations are presented in the operations orders in the appendixes. Comparative analysis has established certain patterns for the scenarios, and those patterns have had a direct effect on the dynamics and outcomes of past exercises.

From the inception of the research, limits were placed on the investigation in order to analyze systematically terrorist incidents that could be simulated. This was essential if the complex factors and issues surrounding the topic of terrorism were to be manageable. The limitations were as follows:

1. It was not the intent of the researchers to cover all types of terrorist incidents. Only incidents involving personal interaction among the terrorists, the victims, and the authorities were to be analyzed. Thus the most common terrorist acts, bombings, were eliminated from consideration because the perpetrators plant the charge and leave the scene before the incidents occur.

2. Only manifestly political incidents were studied. The lines separating criminal terrorism, criminal terrorism with quasi-political content, and political terrorism are often blurred. Thus we eliminated from the study criminal acts in which terror was not employed in a systematic and planned manner, such as hostage-taking accompanying a robbery or a domestic dispute. Political terrorism is characterized by the proclaimed motivation behind the act, the kinds of demands that are made, the target, the response of authorities, and other associated factors.

3. The research was limited primarily to acts with international content as opposed to international impact. Although the line is often blurred, there is quite a difference between acts that have international content because of the nature of the demands, the targets, and other elements and terroristic acts that have international impact because of media coverage.

A preliminary analysis of 111 incidents produced certain key findings which were confirmed by other studies. Those findings established the major principles of scenario building and then the conduct of the entire simulation. The tactical, behavioral, administrative, and policy issues related to those findings will be discussed in detail throughout our analysis of the simulations, but the following overview is useful to set the stage for the development of the scenarios.

Personnel and Logistic Requirements

In the initial analysis it was ascertained that the terrorists were young (average age, twenty-five) and usually male and well armed. Accordingly, in developing the scenario and selecting or recruiting those who played the terrorist, stress was placed on having a terrorist group that roughly approximated the profile. However, to avoid the dangers of stereotyping from undue reliance on profiles, and to test various responses by the reaction forces, deliberate attempts were made to devise scenarios that had women, members of various minorities, and older people in leadership positions.

Care was taken to have the terrorist group armed primarily with semiautomatic and automatic pistols, rifles, and machine guns, since these were commonly the weapons of the terrorist groups studied in the sample. More sophisticated weapons, such as hand-held missile launchers, will be incorporated into the scenarios of future simulations, but, as will be noted, conventionally armed "terrorists" have proved more than a match for even highly trained special-weapons-and-tactics teams from the police and military units participating in the simulations.

The scenarios also took directly into account the personnel requirements that would be recognized by an actual terrorist assault unit. The strike forces in all the exercises varied in number from three to seven, because in most of the incidents examined, the terrorist groups had between two and eight members. Scenarios that stressed small-unit tactics strained the capacity of responding forces to counter the threat and underscored the need for effective intelligence.

In the selection of victims an attempt was made to recruit individuals who had or could be viewed as having political connections or symbolic value. The targeting was based on findings that most victims are diplomats and other government representatives, foreign military personnel, or business executives who are adjudged to be political by the various terrorist groups. In most of the simulations the victims were military personnel, who, because of their affiliation and the requirement that they travel extensively in unsettled areas, bore a high risk of becoming targets. The scenarios provided a realistic setting in which they could learn the behavior patterns that they might experience if they were confronted by an actual attack. Moreover, the simulations enabled them to put into practice lessons in hostage survival techniques.

Two particularly crucial findings from the preliminary analysis were central to the development of all the scenarios. First, in a hostage-taking incident involving negotiation between the terrorists and hostages the first three days are critical for the hostages. Second, terrorists usually do not comply with the time limits they impose at the inception of an incident. Consequently, in developing all the scenarios, an attempt was made to provide an alternative for negotiation if the authorities had both the willingness and the skills to resolve an incident without resort to arms. The simulations, therefore, were a means by which the police could test their hostage negotiation skills in the most realistic setting possible.

From the comparative analysis it was evident that the role of the media was a crucial factor in acts of terrorism. Therefore, in the scenarios the terrorists attempted to publicize their causes. As the terrorists sought to manipulate the media, whose representatives often came to cover the simulations as reporters, not observers, the tensions inherent in police-press relations came to the fore. At the same time, the simulations brought to life the

often-acrimonious debates that characterize the relationship between the media and terrorism.

It was evident from the preliminary findings that few nation-
states develop consistent response strategies when confronted
with an incident. Consequently, while the scenarios were primarily intended to check the responses of civilian and military
law-enforcement agencies, questions relating to policy formulation and execution were also examined. In exercise after exercise the responding units—like nation-states—lacked a consistent policy and therefore let the situation dictate their actions.

Common Elements in the Scenario

Each scenario differed to meet the requirements of the locale
where the simulation took place, the training requirements and
threat assessment of the local jurisdiction, and the research interests of the Study Group. Still certain common elements were
present in all of the scenarios. In part this commonality was
based on the preliminary findings, but of equal significance was
the conscious attempt to build common elements into all the exercises so as to have a standard to evaluate the behavior of the
participants in the various simulations.

The scenarios essentially involved the seizure of hostages by
an overtly political terrorist group. The terrorists, who were
very well armed, made a series of demands that included all or
part of the following: an extremely large ransom, very extensive
publicity for their cause, the freeing of political prisoners, and
an aircraft to take them to an unspecified "progressive" country.
If the demands were not met, the terrorists threatened to kill
the hostages and detonate prepositioned explosives near the
site of the seizure and at various locations in the jurisdiction
where the incident occurred.

The building of the scenario, which provides the framework
for the detailed operations order, went through the phases presented on the following pages.

The Preparatory Phase

In this phase of scenario building the following elements were considered:

The selection of the type of incident and target. All the incidents involved the seizure of hostages, but they differed in other respects. The scenarios might involve the seizure of relatively few hostages with no readily apparent political connections or the seizure of individuals who were highly symbolic and vulnerable targets because of their positions. The target varied from relatively remote facilities to highly visible installations, such as international airports. Whenever possible, the physical target selected was a facility that might actually be subject to attack, but sometimes a potential target was reproduced on the site of the attack because of such problems as crowd and traffic control. The targets selected varied from nonsensitive locations to highly critical and technologically sophisticated installations, such as an oil refinery in the downtown area of a medium-sized city.

The selection of hostages. One simulation involved the seizure of a mock-up of a passenger jet. All the hostages—except the flight attendants, who were undergoing training—were selected randomly. Most scenarios called for specific types of hostages. In the exercises there was a concerted effort to recruit people for the hostage role who were potential targets because of their professions, who, because of their duties, would benefit from learning how it feels to be at the other end of the gun, or who had a direct interest in the study of terrorism. Whenever possible, individuals were chosen who represented the government and traveled extensively. Military personnel who had or would have advisory roles overseas were constantly brought into the scenarios. Members of special-weapons-and-tactics teams and officers who would be designated as hostage negotiators were chosen because, by participating as hostages, they would better appreciate the possible consequences of their actions if they ever had to respond to a real incident.

The motivation and ideological factors behind the incident. Before recruitment or selection of the "terrorists" it was necessary to create the program and related ideology that the assaulting group would use to justify their actions and their demands. In most of the simulations the ideological complexion of the terrorist group was a mixture of left-wing rhetoric and anarchistic positions. The declarations of the group usually consisted of very provocative statements relating to the destruction of the establishment and a call for revolutionary action. The international ties of the terrorist group were continually stressed in statements that the organization was part of a movement that included highly publicized groups, such as the United Red Army and the Red Brigades. The call for action was primarily in terms of exhorting "the masses" to domestic violence. It was constantly implied that the terrorists were part of a larger transnational coalition to indicate that the incident was not simply a local problem.

The selection or recruitment of the terrorists. Great care was given to the selection of the individuals who played the terrorist roles. In the final analysis, the success or failure of the exercises depended on how effectively they carried out their missions and how credible they were as a threat to the hostages and the responding police or military units. When time permitted, individuals were recruited who had participated in past simulations. If the "terrorists" had worked together before, they had had the opportunity not only to refine their techniques through experience but also to develop a degree of cohesiveness as a group that added greatly to the realism of the exercise. In a number of the simulations there was little time for extensive preparation, and the terrorists had not worked together before, but certain guidelines were used in selecting individuals to take on the new and challenging role:

1. There was a systematic attempt to select individuals who had very extensive tactical experience either in their current position or in the past. Stress was placed on recruiting personnel who were trained in the techniques of nonconventional warfare. People who had served or were serving in the Special Forces were particularly effective since they could ably adapt their skills and bring sophisticated tactics associated with urban guerrilla warfare to the simulation. These highly trained tacticians could conduct operations that challenged the most sophisticated responding units. Their threat was credible and placed a heavy burden on the tactical forces who attempted to counter them.

2. Care was taken to recruit individuals who were knowledgable and articulate in presenting radical ideologies. College graduates with extensive interests in political theory played as realistically as possible the disaffected sons and daughters of the establishment who have so often been at the forefront of major terrorist incidents. Their intellectual threats had to be as imposing as the tactical capabilities of their colleagues if they were to be effective in writing the manifestos and stating the demands that are often an integral part of "armed propaganda."

3. A concerted effort was made to induct members of different minority groups and women into the terrorist band in order to match the multiethnic composition of many terrorist bands and reflect the number of actual terrorist incidents in which women have played key roles in the assault force. Perhaps most importantly, the recruitment of minorities and women brought into play a number of interpersonal factors that are crucial in testing the human-relations techniques of both the police and the hostages.

4. Whenever possible, professional actors and others with acting experience were selected for the simulation. The professionals added a great deal to the simulations because they have the training and discipline to utilize techniques of improvisational theater, which may be crucial in bringing a high degree of emotional realism to the exercise.

In this mixture of skills and backgrounds each individual brought into play his respective values, talents, and techniques, and a credible exercise evolved. Yet their ultimate success in providing a tactically refined incident and a politically sophisticated series of demands depended on their abilities as actors. Individually and collectively the terrorists had to get into their roles and convert the scenario into a performance in which the line between acting and terrorizing was lost. The techniques that enabled the terrorists to get into their roles will be discussed in Chapter 6.

The organizational framework. Once the basic outline of the plot, or scenario, had been written, and the actor-terrorists were selected, the organization for the assault began. It was at this time that the terrorists began working together, building their organization and modifying the broad outlines of the scenario into a far more detailed plan, which ultimately became the basis for the operations order. In the days before the operation the terrorists developed a program for action that took into account such problems as the capacities of the responding forces and the acquisition of the necessary arms and related equipment to execute the assault. In addition, manifestos setting out the demands of the group had to be prepared for presentation to the police and the media during the siege.

The Operational Phase

The scenario is refined even further as the terrorist organization begins to deal with the many complex factors surrounding the actual conduct of the operation. At this time the following phases are employed as the basis for establishing the subsequent operations order:

The means of infiltration: breaching security. In developing the scenario, considerable attention had to be given to the techniques that would be used to initiate the action. That concern was, of course, vital if the simulation was to be a success, but

The operational phase. *Courtesy of the Tulsa, Oklahoma, Police Special Hostage Negotiation Teams.*

equally important was that at this stage responding forces can be made aware of deficiencies in measures to prevent an incident from occurring.

Breaching security was not difficult in the simulations because most of the targets selected were nonmilitary in nature. Even when police or private guards are posted at such a locale, their capacity to stop a determined and professionally organized assault is limited. The targets were easily accessible simply because most of the sites were not, and could not be, thoroughly defended. The airports, the refinery, and the other sites of the exercises were chosen in part because they illustrated the great vulnerability of the civil sector to a full assault.

The terrorists were continually assisted in their penetration of different installations because the guards assumed that terrorists would look and act in a certain manner. Stereotypes were often used by the terrorists in developing the scenario. They would maintain a very low profile to penetrate the area where the target was located.

Securing the hostages. As the refinement of the scenario continued, stress was placed on the means by which the hostages would be seized. In each of the simulations the seizures were made in the most unexpected locale possible. The resulting shock and disorientation were essential in forcing the hostages to accept their role as captives and greatly enhanced the realism of the simulations. The responses of the victims to being taken captive will be discussed in detail in Chapter 13.

The communications function. In developing all the scenarios, it was essential that adequate plans be made to develop effective communications with the authorities and with the media. Throughout all the simulations communications with the responding units influenced the outcome of the exercise. Communications problems had important implications for the fate of the hostages. Communications were also of great importance to the terrorists if they were to get their message across to the media. Indeed, effective preparation gave the terrorists an opportunity to manipulate members of the media for their own ends.

Development of potential alternative conclusions. In completing the scenario, the terrorists had to evaluate carefully their possible reactions to the positions taken by the responding forces. Throughout all the simulations the tactical and political options were carefully analyzed so that different conclusions were built into each scenario. The ultimate outcome might be a stalemate, an assault by the responding forces, or the acquiescence by authorities to the terrorists' demands, but while these alternatives were developed, there was a constant recognition that the final outcome should not be scripted since it would depend on how the terrorists, police, hostages, and other involved parties inter-acted. The simulations had to be open-ended to reflect the dy-namics of an actual incident.

With these considerations in mind, the final scenario was constructed, and a terrorist "script" was prepared to set the stage for the simulation.

6 Writing the Terrorist Script

In writing the scripts, or operations orders, for the simulations, adjustments were made to meet the various requirements created by local conditions under which the exercises were carried out. At the same time certain common characteristics were incorporated into each operations order to develop a baseline to compare the responses of the different forces participating in the simulations. The characteristics were modified by each of the terrorists groups, who ultimately wrote their own operations orders for the simulations they initiated, but the following elements were constant in the scripts:

1. The terrorists were primarily highly motivated political activists who were using the incident to promote their causes.

2. The terrorist groups claimed to belong to radical organizations that justified their acts ideologically by employing the extreme left-wing or anarchist rhetoric of transnational terrorist organizations, such as the Baader-Meinhof Gang and the United Red Army. While the terrorists might claim to be primarily a domestic political force, they systematically conveyed the image of links with foreign organizations.

3. In formulating their demands, the terrorists attempted to maximize the impact of their actions by carefully developing manifestos, which indicated that they were members of highly dedicated and politically inspired organizations striking back at the symbols of international repression.

4. In selecting targets, care was taken, whenever possible, to seize installations that were highly visible and consequently would warrant extensive media coverage. The physical targets were often selected because they had symbolic importance that helped not only to justify the terrorist action but also to force the authorities to react with a degree of strength that enhanced the dramatic impact of the seizure. The selection of the hostages was also based, whenever possible, on their positions or affiliations, which further promoted the terrorists' goals. (Some random selection of hostages was also employed to convey the message that no one is safe or innocent in the eyes of terrorists.)

5. In all the simulations the terrorists developed operations orders based on composites of actual incidents: the scripts had to be based on the reality of transnational violence.

The Operations Order

The operations orders essentially adhered to the format employed by the military in planning for small-unit exercises. That format was selected because the lead terrorist in most of the exercises had extensive military experience. It also affirmed the presence in the terrorist band of skilled professionals well equipped to engage in a sophisticated assault. The basic elements of the order were placed under the following headings.

Situation. The situation establishes the name and organization of the group that are engaging in the act of terrorism. Under this heading are included a brief history of the organization and its past operations and the composition of its membership, as well as its organizational framework and its location. The political ideology and the general goals of the terrorist group are also related in this section. The development of this part of the order provides the terrorists an opportunity to establish their organizational affiliation and identity. It also enables all of them to get more quickly into the personal roles that they will play throughout the preparation and duration of the simulation.

In developing the organizational framework, political complexion, composition, and goals of the terrorist organization, care is taken to reproduce the characteristics of actual groups—both domestic and international—and modify them to local conditions. There is no attempt to reproduce an actual group because the individual terrorists would then assume artificial roles instead of building their own organizational identity. Furthermore, if the name of an actual group were used during a simulation, there would be the remote possibility that observers who were not informed that a simulation was in progress would react as if a real threat existed.

The Mission. Once their organizational identity is established, the terrorists begin to function as a group. It is time to formulate their missions. In virtually all the exercises the attacks were initiated by a small band who were well trained and heavily armed. They utilized their small numbers as a means of achieving mobility and clandestine capabilities to neutralize or penetrate whatever security measures had been established to protect the target. As in actual terrorist groups the operations order did not contain the names and locations of the headquarters personnel. Such information is given only to the leader of the assault. The leader has the only liaison with his or her immediate superiors. The organizational chain of command is deliberately not written into the mission because such information is dispensed only on a need-to-know basis. Thus the terrorist cell remains distinct from the larger organization, which is protected in the event that the assault force is compromised or captured.

In defining the mission, the date of the attack, the targets, and other pertinent information must be presented. In addition, the forces that can be expected to respond are evaluated. This intelligence information is obtained not only from the members of the assault group but also from sympathetic support personnel, who may have found relatively deep cover in the area where the attack will take place. Furthermore, there is a concerted effort to obtain information from members of the local law-enforcement community.

Execution. Once the mission is defined, a detailed plan of attack is developed. Such a plan includes the kinds of demands that will be made and the means by which they will be communicated to both the authorities and the media. In preparing the demands, the ideologists of the assault unit, in conjunction with the other terrorists, often prepare a detailed manifesto to have it ready for distribution at the inception of the attack. In addition to the preparation of the manifesto, great care is given to establishing the tactical and logistical requirements of the operation. The types of weapons that will be employed, the means to which the target will be held, the requirements for additional equipment, including scanners to break the security of the police radio net, are subjected to detailed analysis. Such basic requirements as independent sources of food and water—to neutralize the authorities' basis for negotiations—are carefully assessed and stored. The terrorist organization attempts to be as self-sufficient as possible.

In preparing for an assault against a high-technology target, such as an oil refinery, an appendix may be written into the operations order describing special techniques that can be used to maximize the destructive capabilities of the terrorists so as to strengthen their threat credibility and their negotiating hand with authorities. The authors of such an appendix are usually trained engineers or scientists who have the knowledge to turn the technology of modern society against itself.[1] These "techno-guerrillas"[2] may be actual members of the assault force directing the technical scenario, or they may be support members of the organization who will not be involved in the actual attack.

Finally, different choices in escape and evasion techniques are incorporated into the execution section of the operations order. Some crucial requirements, for instance, the need for transportation and safe housing, are the subjects of contingency planning in the event that the assault is a failure or the authorities refuse to meet the demands on them.

As in a conventional, or nonconventional, war, the terrorist operation calls for a degree of preparedness that is characteristic of a military operation. This is to be expected, for the terrorists perceive themselves to be soldiers in their own declared war against the social order.

Supplemental Administrative Order

In addition to the operations order that is written and followed by the terrorists, a supplemental order is prepared by the simulation director and the terrorists and shared with the responding authorities. This order establishes crucial guidelines that must be adhered to by all the participants in the simulation. It includes such items as the safety rules and the means by which the exercise will be evaluated. This administrative scenario is presented in Chapter 8.

7 Preparing for Violence
Getting into the Role

The writing of the operations order by the would-be terrorists assists them in physically preparing for the assault. It also prepares them for a simulation by helping them individually and collectively to assume their roles emotionally. This kind of assumption of the role is essential if the terrorists are going to go beyond simply playing at being potential murderers. They must begin to identify with each other as members of a highly motivated group who are willing to risk their lives for a common cause. Only when that identification occurs do the individuals involved not only act but also *think* and *feel* as if they have entered the underground world of contemporary terrorism. This need for identification is vital, for, unless the terrorists totally assume their roles, they run the risk of playing at them and of becoming little more than stereotypes. The resulting charade will destroy the effectiveness of the simulation.

Playing at Terrorism Is Not Enough

If the simulation terrorists do not move beyond superficial appearances and actions, their performance in the simulation will bear little or no relation to the actions of the real terrorists who are waging their undeclared war on authority in the world today. If the terrorists in the exercise do not work at developing their physical and emotional capacities to challenge the responding forces, they will not be a credible threat. Unless identification takes place, they lack the commitment that must exist if the negotiators, field commanders, and other concerned personnel are to be forced to acknowledge that they are dealing with a dedicated band and that the responding units cannot simply play in an antiterrorist exercise. By being a dedicated, credible tactical group, the terrorists can force the responding personnel at all levels to "suspend" their disbelief and force them physically and emotionally to accept that the line between a drill and reality is blurred. This acceptance is also essential for those on the other side of the barricade. If the terrorists play their roles effectively, the hostages will begin to realize both emotionally and intellectually that they are, indeed, victims whose lives are subject to negotiation.

In order to help the terrorists to assume their roles, several techniques are employed individually and collectively within the constraints on time and on the availability of personnel for a given simulation.

At the inception of planning for the simulation, each of the prospective terrorists is asked to write his or her personal history. Samples of the biographical data obtained appear in the appendixes. The creation of the terrorist's identity in the simulation in part reflects the actual life experience of the simulator so that the historical factors are consistent with his upbringing and personality. There is, therefore, a concerted attempt to prevent members of the band from engaging in fantasies by developing backgrounds that have no relationship to their actual family upbringings and economic and social status. With this limitation the terrorists can assume their roles more comfortably. They should not attempt to create identities more in keeping with "The Secret Life of Walter Mitty" than with their own upbringings. Thus, for example, if a young, upper-middle-class male from a small middle-western town tries to establish a past history based on being brought up in an urban, lower-class setting, the identity is flawed. Creation of the terrorist family history calls for an exercise in imagination, but it must be consistent with the experience of the individual who is creating it.

Additional constraints are placed on the writing of the history and the creation of an identity by the scenario: the individual identities that are created must be consistent with the demands imposed by the forthcoming exercise. Thus, for example, if one of the individuals is recruited because of a specialized skill that is essential for an operation, the means by which the skill was acquired must be integrated into the personal dossier. Conversely, the members of the group must not claim skills that they do not possess. One individual, for example, might wish to claim that he had extensive military background that could be used in the operation, but, unless that claim can be backed up by actual experience, it cannot be incorporated into the personal history. There is also an attempt to select individuals who, because of their educational background, social or economic class, profession, and other related factors, have the attributes that are found in the various profiles of terrorists. Again, care is taken to avoid the dangers of stereotyping and to insist that the factors that are incorporated into the background data of each terrorist reflect, at least in part, his or her real experience. On the basis of these considerations each individual writes a biography that provides the main historical elements of the identity that he or she will assume before, during, and even after the simulation. The data include the revolutionary code names that will be employed throughout the operation.

In writing the biographical data, each individual provides only the information that he or she wishes to be made public to the other members of the band. This uneven availability of data reflects in part the personalities of the participants. Significant omissions will be filled in as the terrorists get to know each other.

Most of the participants in the various simulations are college-educated, are from middle-class backgrounds, have extensive military experience, and are, with exceptions, in their twenties and thirties. Thus the biographical data indicate a degree of commonality among all the terrorists. To a degree, a profile of the terrorists in the simulations is unintentionally developed. Still, despite the shared elements, the autobiographies reflect the unique experiences and personalities of their authors.

The data serve another purpose. In written form the biographies can provide valuable intelligence to the responding forces if they know how to acquire and analyze them. By this means one aspect of the participating police or military units' intelligence capabilities can be evaluated.

The data take on life only when the terrorists assume their personalities during the interaction as they prepare to strike the target. The fusion of the data to the personality of the individual who is assuming a terrorist role and identity can be a gradual process if there is adequate time for the members of the organization to work together. Whenever possible, the members of the group meet as many times as possible before the exercise to get to know each other's new identity and, perhaps more important, so that each can assume his or her own role. When there was an opportunity, as there was in a number of simulations, to prepare for weeks before the operation, the assumptions of the terrorist roles by the participants were often quite impressive. Even when the terrorists have only a few days to put their new identities into action, identification takes place in a remarkably short time, since the individuals are only modifying their own background to a new, if unfamiliar, set of circumstances. This assumption of a role stands in marked contrast to the war-game exercise, where the participants play a part only superficially instead of relating emotionally to an assumed identity.

The assumption of the individual identities takes on a collective meaning as the terrorists work together on the mission of the organization in which they find themselves. While the broad framework for the organization is in the scenario, the group will not become an organic, functioning unit until the participants bring it to life as they prepare for the operation. The political complexion, the hierarchy, and the factors associated with the operation of any small organization, including a terrorist group, are refined as the organization prepares for its mission.

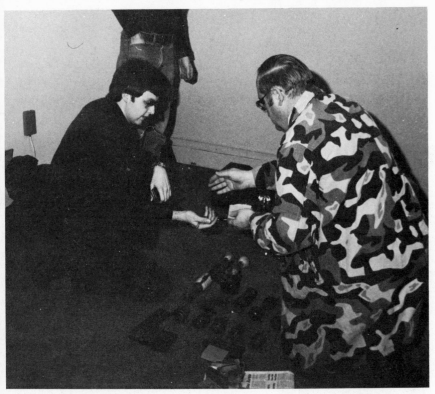

Preparing for the assault. *Courtesy of the Tulsa, Oklahoma, Police Special Hostage Negotiation Teams.*

The development of the political ideology of the terrorist band and the related demands upon authorities are the products of group decisions in most instances. Even here leadership emerges from individuals who are conversant with the rhetoric of radical politics or with other members of the terrorist group who have the ability to write effectively. For example, in one exercise one of the rhetoricians was a professional writer whose best-selling novels included plots associated with terrorist incidents.

The specialized skills of the recruits are utilized, particularly when the target is a high-technology installation. In the seizure of an oil refinery, for example, a petroleum engineer was recruited into the band so that his skills could be utilized against the plant.

Despite this specialization of function, it must be stressed that, as in actual incidents, all the terrorists are trained in the rudiments of handling weapons, seizing hostages, and the other essential military skills that must be employed in a successful operation. As in any actual small-scale operation terrorists cannot afford the luxury of separating the staff functions from the line functions. The absence of specialization is one way that they differ from the responding forces.

The organization takes on further identity when women and various minority groups are deliberately recruited. This recruitment is meant in part to reflect the multiethnic composition that has been noted on occasion in terrorist groups. It also creates an interesting diversity of outlook among the organization's members, who must develop cohesiveness for the impending simulation. The selection of different nationality groups and women is meant primarily to create crucial problems in human relationships, which must be handled by the responding forces, particularly the hostage negotiators, during the conduct of the simulation.

Finally, there is a conscious policy of not selecting individuals to play the roles of terrorists in the simulations who are members of police forces or who have extensive law-enforcement experience. In too many of the exercises conducted among the police and the military, personnel from the same profession or units played the role of terrorists. The exercises were often flawed because the terrorists spoke the same language and shared many values with the forces they were engaging. Moreover, many of them may actually have returned to duty and work with the very hostages they "captured" or with the same police they challenged. In such cases participants in the exercise may lack the perspective that is necessary if the supposed terrorists are to test the capacity of the responding forces effectively. Because, in actual life, terrorists reject the society in which they find themselves, particularly the forces of law and order, they do not share the values of the forces that are marshaled against them. Therefore, in a simulation the terrorists should not come from the very organizations they are to attack. In preparation for the simulation the terrorists must turn their backs on the social order because they are to play outsiders who cannot be a part of it. They are not members of the law-enforcement community.

As the individual terrorists assume their identities and develop a collective consciousness, the preparation for the planned assault ideally should transform each of them from a person playacting as a terrorist to a terrorist preparing to initiate an operation in which, for the duration of the simulation, he believes in and to which he is committed even if the outcome ends in bloodshed. Thus an emotional stage is set for the physical attack.

8 Planning for Violence
Administrative Concerns

In preparing for a simulation, many administrative details must be taken care of if the program is ultimately to be effective. There must be attention to detail, because even the most elementary simulation calls for extensive planning to meet the training requirements of the sponsoring jurisdiction and the research agenda of the study group. Furthermore, while each exercise is open-ended, it is vital that care is taken to ensure effective safety measures. A successful simulation entails a high degree of realism and tension. There must be guidelines so that all the participants recognize certain limits in their roles without sacrificing the uncertainty that should be inherent in each program.

In the evolution of each simulation there is a concerted attempt to develop a scenario that will meet the training requirements of the participating departments or units. In all the exercises the responding authorities have been particularly interested in the training and evaluation of their hostage-negotiation teams and special-weapons-and-tactics units. Beyond those concerns, the scenarios are fashioned to meet the kind of threat that the department anticipates in its jurisdiction. Thus the selection of targets and accompanying demands are customized. In Tulsa, Oklahoma, the responding forces shared a concern that oil refineries within their jurisdiction were potential sites for incidents. In another simulation the possible seizure of aircraft represented an ongoing concern among the authorities. The simulators must be sensitive to the local factors that condition responses in the participating jurisdiction. While the character of the terrorist group, the selection of the target, and the method of assault can come from outside the jurisdiction or can be inspired by an external group, certain local conditions remain constant and place various constraints on the responding forces irrespective of the kind of incident. The availability of targets, the composition and training of the participating units, and the administrative-political structures that would figure in an actual incident place important limits on the scenario.

Once the framework of the scenario is agreed to by the commanding officers of the police or military forces, the senior personnel are no longer involved in the development of the simulation if they are actually going to be in command of their forces when the incident is initiated. As in an actual crisis they must develop their response without any prior knowledge of the terrorist assault. Cooperation with senior commanders is, of course, vital to ensure that the exercise meets the requirements of their departments, but the commanding officer, like his personnel, must be kept in the dark about the details of the impending operation if he or she is going to participate in the decision-making process once the simulation begins. An officer is selected to act as a liaison to assist the study group in obtaining the equipment, selecting personnel, and other preparations for the attack. Only the liaison officer will be given a copy of the operations order for the simulation, which is classified, so that he can assist the study group in meeting the preexercise requirements. Security in the development of each simulation is vital, and distribution of the operations order is strictly on a need-to-know basis.

The liaison officer is essential also because of a wide variety of requirements that must be attended to before the simulation can be successfully executed. The following areas are of particular concern in preparing for the exercise.

Personnel Requirements

Whenever possible, the recruitment of the terrorists takes place without the knowledge or cooperation of officers in the jurisdiction. Even when the terrorists are recruited in the area where the exercise is to take place, the selection process often depends on the contacts of the study group. Thus, for example, in one exercise the lead terrorist—at that time a captain in a U.S. Army Special Forces Reserve—recruited three noncommissioned officers who served with a detachment in the city where the simulation occurred.

In some cases the recruitment process must be carried out locally and in a very short period of time. When this is so, it is usually not difficult to find individuals with the requisite training in nonconventional warfare if the simulation is to take place for a military unit. It should be stressed that the selection process is kept secret from the responding authority because of the need for a clandestine operation. In addition, it is not difficult to obtain other terrorists with particular talents that can be employed for the exercise. In one instance individuals with acting experience were found through a college drama department in the area, and other individuals were found who had experience in community theater. This recruitment process, while not as systematic as the one to be employed if there is sufficient lead time, nevertheless can produce individuals with highly relevant backgrounds. In one exercise a foreign-service officer with experience both in U.S. State Department security and in acting was able to fuse his experiences to become a first-rate terrorist. In a sense, local recruitment simply reflects the disturbing fact that there are people in many locales with the training to be terrorists who might find involvement in an actual incident too compelling to pass up. Although their numbers may be small, in any large urban area the recruitment process is not difficult. The skills are always there. A considerable number of individuals have had extensive military experience or have a knowledge of weapons. Politically motivated would-be terrorists clearly represent a very small portion of the population, but they can be reached. Potential terrorists do not simply live in another town.

Arms and Associated Equipment

Perhaps even more disturbing than the ready availability of trained personnel to take on the terrorists' roles is the ease with which one can acquire and transport the arms, ammunition, and related equipment that are used in a simulation but also would be employed in an actual incident. Obviously, when the simulation is conducted for the military, the acquisition of weapons is relatively easy, but even in such instances the simulators often bring with them pistols and rifles not readily available on the site that are clearly a part of the terrorist arsenal. These additions have included M-16 rifles, German machine pistols, M-1 carbines, AK-47s, and other stock not commonly found in conventional military arsenals. When working with the police, it is usually necessary to provide the weapons because most departments rely primarily on shotguns and have only recently acquired automatic and semiautomatic weapons. In most instances the terrorist band can be equipped with a wider variety and a potentially more destructive series of weapons than the arsenal of the police whom they will face.

The terrorists, whether they acquire their equipment on the site or bring it with them, are prepared to utilize a full arsenal in addition to rifles, pistols, and machine guns. Before an operation the terrorists bring with them or obtain locally training hand grenades, simulated plastic explosives, and other supplemental weapons to make their threat highly credible. Many kinds of booby traps are often fashioned. Examples have ranged from spring-triggered land mines to a device that would automatically have electrocuted a hostage if a door was opened. The latter infernal device was prepared by an electrical engineer using his skills in a way that he never expected.

Small training aids are often fabricated that either detonate or blow a whistle before and during the simulation. The detonation of a smoke bomb at the beginning of a simulation serves excellently to bring realism to the exercise and also as a warning that the terrorists are very well armed.

Finally, a great deal of supplemental equipment is acquired by the terrorist group. This includes devices that are available to the public, such as scanners to break the security of the responding forces' ratio net and classified military manuals. The preparation also requires basic equipment, such as handcuffs, plastic tape, and bags to place over the hostages' heads.

The acquisition of the weapons was a relatively easy task in all the simulations. What was particularly impressive was that, even without the cooperation of participating military or police units, there was no shortage of semiautomatic and automatic weapons available from private sources. Gun collectors, veterans, and other individuals were of great help in providing semiautomatic weapons that could be readily transformed into automatic operation. In addition, a wide variety of training aids, ranging from grenade launchers to mines, can be secured easily on the open market. Also, by using either their academic training or a wide variety of training manuals, the terrorists, if they desired, could readily make their own demolition devices.[1]

If it is disturbing to recognize the availability of weapons in preparing for a simulation, it is equally vexing to recognize how easily the weapons can be transported even where there appears to be a security screen or at least basic security measures. In all the exercises, even where the essential weapons were acquired at the site of the simulation, some weapons and related equipment were transported. Although prior notification was given in some instances, it was still easy to transport an extensive arsenal across the country without even bothering to notify authorities. Furthermore, the transportation of such equipment is perfectly legal. Since it is not the intent of this book to compromise security at various installations, details of how readily security measures can be ignored or breached will not be presented; however, the fact remains that at civilian locales, at certain private installations, and even at military installations, the introduction of weapons is not difficult. This is particularly apparent in the security at public installations, where it is essential that the private security personnel, as well as the local police, reevaluate their capacity to provide at least a modicum of secure perimeters in the areas under their jurisdiction and control.

Bureaucratic Concerns and Infighting

Once the logistical requirements are satisifed, the next administrative priority is to provide means by which the responding authority can evaluate its bureaucratic capacities—as opposed to its more obvious tactical capacities—through the simulation technique.

At the inception of planning, care is taken to ascertain not only what unit or units will be involved but also the degree of command involvement in either a jurisdictional or multijurisdictional setting. In most of the earlier exercises the chain of command was limited essentially to the responding units in the field. Thus at the inception of the simulation the players consisted primarily of the tactical unit, which included the hostage-negotiation team under the direction of a field-grade officer. The officer was usually a lieutenant or captain in the police or a captain or major in the military. Such exercises provided effective training for the field forces, but they failed to provide a means by which the higher command—those who would be responsible if a real terrorist incident occurred—could be tested in the techniques of crisis management. Whenever possible, senior commanders were asked if they wished to participate directly instead of just observing the simulations. Because of time constraints, financial factors, and related conditions, it was only in the later exercises that the higher command, to the level of chief of police, actually took charge in the command post. Even in those exercises the capacity to evaluate command and control was limited because the exercises did not include the senior civilian officials, such as commissioners and elected officers, who in the final analysis make the ultimate decisions in a jurisdiction under stress. The seriousness of that limitation was further aggravated: in most of the simulations, even when relatively senior officers participated, their administrative capabilities could not be fully tested because the participating forces did not represent the various jurisdictions and organizations that would respond to an actual incident. In a number of the later exercises personnel from different organizations were involved, but only as individuals, not as representatives of their organizations. Consequently, in developing exercises that truly test the administrative response to an incident, it would be ideal if all the senior officials were mobilized along with their staffs from all the organizations that would be in key decision-making positions in actual incidents. In this manner the levels of interdepartmental coordination and cooperation could be evaluated under stress as they should be. In an incident of politically motivated terrorism involving well-armed terrorists with international demands, a task force has to be created almost instantaneously. The ability of such a force to fight the terrorists instead of engaging in bureaucratic infighting is best tested in an exercise where the flaws of the contingency plans—if any—are tested. Aspects of administrative behavior and its implications for more effective crisis management will be discussed in Chapter 12.

Safety Measures

Throughout the preparation for the simulations emphasis is continually placed on developing correct safety measures. Achieving a high degree of realism calls for the use of blank ammunition and detonating devices. It is essential that a safety officer clearly establish ground rules that will be followed by all the participants. The emotional states of the hostages, the terrorists, and the responding forces produce a level of anxiety and tension that is extremely dangerous when weapons—even blanks—are handled. It is vital to sensitize all participants to basic safety measures without developing a list of operational requirements that detracts from the realism necessary to enable the performers to get into their roles. The means by which safety consciousness can be developed without interfering with the suspension of disbelief will be presented in the next chapter.

9 Briefing Before Violence
Reconciling Realism and Safety

In initiating a simulation, care must be taken to reconcile the need for surprise and realism with adequate safety measures. Consequently, in the briefings that are conducted before each exercise certain ground rules are established. The same precautions are taken irrespective of the kind of seizure or the location of the simulation.

Immediately before the exercise the participants who are not members of the responding forces are notified that they will be involved in a training exercise in which some of them will be taken hostage while others will be assigned different roles. In reality, in most instances, all the participants are seized unless before the final briefing they have been given specialized tasks that they are required to keep secret. If the terrorists plan to seize the hostages during the briefing, they may be present at the final meeting, but ordinarily the terrorists are not present during the presentation.

The guidelines for the potential hostages are kept simple and explicit to avoid any possible misunderstandings. The participants are told that, if they are seized, under no circumstances should they attempt to employ force to effect their escape. They are cautioned not to fake either a physical illness or a mental breakdown as a means of attempting to be released from captivity. They are then notified that, if an emergency does take place, it has been preplanned and acted out by selected persons, who are thus testing the responses of the authorities and the terrorists to the crisis. A clear warning is given that, if an undesignated individual fakes an illness, it must be assumed that the emergency is real: the simulation will consequently have to be temporarily suspended or terminated. That requirement is essential because, even though the would-be hostages are in good physical condition, there is no guarantee that physical and mental difficulties will not be experienced by some of them, given the levels of stress that are incorporated into the exercises. Despite the warning, in a number of simulations there was the possibility of overreaction by hostages who thought that one of their fellow victims was ill even though intellectually they knew that the emergency was preplanned. Because of the potentially dangerous emotional responses among individuals in the target group, the simulation director and an observor constantly monitor the emotional climate in the barricaded area during the simulation. If tensions become too intense, the lead terrorist reduces the level of intimidation experienced by the hostages.

The individuals at the briefing are also notified that, if they are taken hostage, they may be subject to high levels of verbal abuse, some physical manhandling, and a degree of physical discomfort. Despite this warning, in virtually all the simulations they were not mentally prepared for what they would experience at the beginning and throughout the simulation. Such a reaction is understandable, since the intense realism of the simulation forces people to accept the roles that they are victims of an actual terrorist assault.

The participants are also informed that, except for the constraints described, they can adopt any role they wish to assume during the exercise. In reality the role playing usually ceases as the hostages are forced to react naturally and adjust intuitively to the situation confronting them.

The hostages are required to give any weapons on their persons, including pocket knives, to a designated officer in the briefing area. This precaution is taken, even though a full and highly professional search is conducted by the terrorists at the inception of the simulation, to avoid the possibility that a would-be victim might smuggle in a weapon and create an incident. During the search in several of the briefings it was interesting to see the variety of supplemental weapons carried by the police.

To provide the element of surprise that will shock the hostages and force them to accept the reality of the situation, different ruses are used to keep them off guard and unprepared for being captured. In two incidents the participants were told to board a bus that would take them to the site where the various roles were to be assigned and the exercise was to be conducted. They were caught off guard when armed terrorists firing blank ammunition seized them as the bus began moving to the training locale. In other exercises the hostages were seized by an armed band as they sat through a very dry lecture on negotiation techniques that was meant to lull them into a relaxed and bored state. They were particularly ill prepared for the shock when the lecture took place after lunch, as some of the audience were nodding off to sleep. Other subterfuges are also employed. In one instance, at a university airport, the individuals selected as hostages were notified that they had won a free vacation trip, given luggage, and sent to the operations room that simulated the waiting room. Only as they arrived at the terminal were they seized by the waiting terrorists. They then embarked on a vastly different type of physical and mental voyage of self-discovery.

The participating units are notified simply that they will be taking part in a training exercise. Details about the type of training are not discussed. Before the exercise is initiated, all the weapons that they carry are checked to ensure that there are no rounds inadvertently left in the chamber.

With the final preparations completed, the stage is set for the impending act of terrorism.

10 Launching the Assault

Forcing People to Think the Unthinkable and Accept It

In all the simulations provisions were made for assessment of the emotional and intellectual responses of the participants. After the earlier simulations this was done primarily through informal discussions at the conclusion of the exercises. In the later programs all the participants, from the hostages to the police, were requested to record their feelings immediately after the conclusion of the simulations. By having each person give his or her impressions right after the exercise, two goals were accomplished. First, the participants were not given the time to intellectualize their feelings or rationalize their behavior, and they could not compare notes with the other persons involved in the simulation. The responses of those who were required to respond immediately were far more candid and intuitive than the reactions of participants who had time to reflect on their experiences. Second, in writing their impressions immediately after the simulation, the participants still had a sense of intimacy with the events in which they had been involved. Indeed, many were still at least partly in their roles as hostages, terrorists, police, members of the media, and so on. They often recorded their emotions as if they were still involved in a terrorist incident instead of redefining their views as they would after time for introspection. To make the participants feel more secure in expressing their true feelings, they were required to note only the positions they held during the exercise; they were not asked to give their names. It was also emphasized that the impressions would be held in confidence and not shared directly with other members of the simulation.

It was interesting to see how different the public pronouncements often were from the private impressions. In many instances the hostages and others asserted after the exercise that they were not intimidated by the terrorists, had constantly kept in mind that they were involved only in a simulation, and essentially had been able to respond effectively to the situation in which they found themselves. The members of the responding forces also would often adopt a public posture stressing that they had the situation under control and could have employed their tactical skill to counter the terrorists. Still, despite a degree of braggadocio, many of the participants were very candid in their public remarks and stimulated discussions that enabled individuals to go beyond a facade of self-confidence, which was primarily meant for public consumption. When the simulations were filmed, some of the participants were interviewed immediately after the exercise, and they often were exceedingly candid in front of the camera. In the final analysis the written impressions and private discussions best captured how each individual felt during the simulations. The macho remarks that were made before the assembled group at the debriefing were replaced by highly sensitive responses from individuals who recognized that the exercise enabled them to discover to some degree how they responded under stress and possibly would respond in a real incident.

The best way to convey how the hostages responded to the initial seizure is simply to note their impressions:

There was an initial shock as the incident developed on the bus. A feeling of helplessness was there because the terrorists took control.

It was a real surprise to find myself taken as a hostage while boarding the bus. The terrorists were very professional and had good control of the hostages from the very beginning.

Initially, on the bus, it was tough getting into the role, but as we drove some nonspecific anxieties began. Then, when they spread-

Terrorism is an equal-opportunity employer. *Courtesy of Port of Portland, Oregon, Police Department.*

A bus trip to possible oblivion: a journey to self-discovery. *Courtesy of Port of Portland, Oregon, Police Department.*

eagled me at the building and the shakes started from holding the position so long, the role acceptance just sort of happened.

Initially shocked on the bus—was not expecting a confrontation that soon.

As the exercise first started, I experienced some anxiety. This combined with the physical discomfort to produce disorientation.

As a hostage I initially found myself in an agitated state as a result of the wild and obnoxious manner in which the terrorists took over the bus and began shooting wildly inside the bus.

The initial impression was that of being overwhelmed.

As a hostage I felt from the start that I was completely under the control of my captors. No decision was left to me.

As a hostage I felt absolutely powerless.

These responses were characteristic of most of the hostages in the different simulations. With few exceptions the individuals who were seized were forced to accept emotionally and intellectually their roles as prisoners. Moreover, the initial shock and disorientation that many of them felt corresponded to the emotional state recorded in actual incidents of hostage-taking. The manner in which the hostages adjusted to being held captive as the simulations went beyond the early stages will be discussed in Chapter 13.

If the hostages were forced to think the unthinkable and accept it, their responses were largely the result of the terrorists' ability to present to their captives a credible mental and physical threat. As noted earlier, the terrorists had already assumed their individual and collective identities as they worked together before the actual operation. Although they were mindful of the need to adhere to safety measures as they initiated the assault, they were not playing at, but increasingly identifying with, their new status. The identification was not solely the result of previous preparation. Immediately before the start of the simulation and during the early phases of the attack, the terrorists actually experienced the tension that grips people who are about to embark on an uncertain and dangerous course of action. Even though the terrorists had the initiative, the reality of the impending operation forced them to accept their roles in much the same way as their reluctant victims, who initially thought that they were simply going to participate in another training exercise. The following impressions underscore the degree of tension experienced by the terrorists when the assaults were launched:

> Before the incident began I was extremely hyper waiting for the action to begin. I was apprehensive when delays caused a change in schedule. I was concerned with controlling twenty-three captives until they could be bound and placed under guard inside the building. Initially I felt I could kill one or all of the hostages without any guilt feeling at all.

> Took tremendous energy. Remember being worried about the initial takeover and could we control them—so exerted much force initially—was surprised that they were so weak and cooperative.

> My role was Geronimo, a character who was a dedicated and sometimes crazy terrorist. The character was one of loyalty, dedication, craziness, and glamor because it allowed me to become a renegade easily. To become Geronimo all that was required was a mission and for the exercise to begin. The rest naturally came in place. I wanted to shoot all the hostages.

This degree of tension was present throughout the simulations. It reinforced the sense of a common reality shared by the terrorists and the hostages alike and impelled them to play out their roles as the siege began.

The emotional responses of the individuals who were to counter the terrorists or cover the story were naturally not as strong as those of the individuals within the barricade, in part because the outsiders had not directly experienced the shock of being taken hostage. In addition, as in actual incidents, there was a very uneven communications pattern, and many of the responding forces were not immediately informed that a crisis had started in their jurisdiction. Deprived of the intimate experience of being captured, it took a longer time for the commanders, hostage negotiators, tactical teams, and other involved parties to get into their roles. As the simulation continued and the pressures began to build, even those who attempted to remain detached often became caught up in the realism of the pro-

Life at the other end of the gun. *Courtesy of the Port of Portland, Oregon, Police Department.*

There is no dignity in a body search. *Courtesy of the Tulsa, Oklahoma, Police Special Hostage Negotiation Teams.*

tracted exercises. The responses on the perimeter and in the command post would increasingly be characterized by a level of anxiety almost as strong as the feelings shared by the terrorists and the hostages.

On the Other Side of the Barricade

Various patterns of individual and collective behavior were replicated in virtually all of the simulations. Those patterns are also seen in actual incidents, and therefore the simulations helped sensitize the police or military personnel to problems that they might experience at the start of a real hostage-taking.

When the initial seizures were completed, the police were often unwilling to accept that a terrorist operation was being conducted in their jurisdiction. Even though all the participants were notified that they would be involved in a training exercise, the shock and surprise of the initial assault carried over to the police, who did not expect the level of professionalism and realism that characterized the initiation of the crisis. This attitude of disbelief prevailed in part because almost none of the officers had been involved in dealing with a terrorist incident or expected that one could take place in their locale. Despite the growing awareness of potential terrorist threats, the police forces in particular did not anticipate that individually or collectively they would be subject to either a training exercise or an actual incident involving what one chief of police referred to as "super-violence."[1] As we shall see, this assumption that it cannot happen here often creates conditions that delay the responses of the units involved in the exercise. The same delayed responses are also observed when military units are participating, but the delays are probably not so much the result of disbelief.

Willingness to accept that a terrorist attack was under way was in part the result of two related factors. First, the various security forces had as one of their major missions the protection of installations against well-equipped and heavily armed hostile forces. The Air and Military Police and, to a degree, the Special Forces Units who were involved in the various simulations were responsible for meeting both conventional and unconventional attacks. In contrast, with the exception of specialized units, who were equipped to respond primarily to hostage-taking and barricade situations that result from a crime and are not politically motivated, most of the police did not have it as their mission to counter a quasi-military force. Second, because of their orientation, virtually none of the police—again with the partial exception of the Special Weapons and Tactics Teams—had undergone a degree of small-unit training for a military operation. In contrast, the personnel from the security forces were continually subjected to exercises to respond to an armed incursion. Those differences in role helped explain their relative willingness to acknowledge that a coercive attack had been launched. Perhaps far more significantly, they raised serious questions of policy about what level of military training and equipment should be given to civilian law-enforcement units to meet a potential threat.

In addition to unwillingness to accept that an assault was under way, the early phases of virtually all the simulations were marked by disorganization and confusion among the responding units. The following impressions of participants aptly illustrate the confusion that prevails throughout a simulation:

While being involved in this exercise I felt inadequate—which was caused greatly by lack of training—and confused as to whether or not the personnel understood their personnel assignments. To much confusion in the command post in general.

From the beginning of the exercise it seemed as though the civilian authorities completely forgot about the eight military members that had surrounded the building. Our personnel had no idea as to what personnel were in the area and what positions they had.

This confusion resulted from surprise at being confronted by incidents that were, for the most part, beyond the experience or training of the responding forces. It raised crucial questions about the development and effective utilization of administrative procedures to meet a potential threat. The problems related to administration are dealt with in Chapter 11.

Because of the degree of realism that characterized all the simulations, other groups were subject to disorientation at the inception of the assault and throughout the exercises. For example, when the media representatives came to cover the crisis, they too, individually and collectively, experienced some of the confusion and shock that the hostages and the police became familiar with as the exercises progressed. The resulting strains at times tested the capacity of the police to maintain good relations with the press. See Chapter 15.

With the simulation under way, most of the participants either willingly or reluctantly assumed their roles. In many cases they were able to experience how it feels to be involved in a siege. Certainly their experiences transcended the sanitized and edited television police programs, which do not prepare viewers to understand the frustration, fear, and boredom that accompany actual incidents. As people were forced to accept their roles, they began to understand a different reality about terrorism.

11 Tensions in the Command Post
The Police Are Also Hostages

In all the simulations, while the victims awaited their uncertain fate, the responding police forces and military units attempted to replace a reactive, emotive response with administrative techniques and related tactical measures to manage the siege. By utilizing contingency plans, drawing on past experience, or both, the field commanders either systematically or intuitively attempted to evolve their own form of "crisis management."

The term *crisis management* has only recently been employed in reference to incidents of terrorism. It denotes a process whereby those in authority learn how to play a potentially deadly game in order to deal with a crisis. As one definition notes:

> We use the term "crisis management" to mean any process which a manager exercises to meet his goals within a potentially deteriorating situation at an acceptable cost to him, persuading those with whom he is interacting that the costs of opposing him are greater than the costs of allowing him to obtain his objective.[1]

Beyond the complex element of gaming inherent in the process is a series of organizational techniques that can be employed to assist decision makers in handling terrorist incidents. The techniques have been increasingly refined and utilized by executives who are responsible for protecting their corporations in the face of the increasing possibility that they may be attractive targets. As Daniel E. Shaffer notes:

The responsibilities of command: pressure in the command post.

Crisis management can be addressed advantageously by a Crisis Management Team (CMT). The CMT should consist of a group of senior management personnel who have the authority to make decisions for the entire corporation during a crisis. Because a small unit is generally capable of reaching decisions more quickly, [it] should consist of the least number of individuals . . . possible.[2]

While Special Agent Shaffer correctly notes that the techniques, when employed by a business, are "not designed as a substitute for law enforcement . . . but rather a complementary support process," they can be modified to meet the requirements of the military and police in dealing with a crisis.

When the crisis-management approach is modified and applied to the law-enforcement community, there are valid questions concerning limitations that may be found in the technique.

First, one can question the advisability of establishing a special organizational framework separate from the routines that are employed to deal with criminals engaged in ordinary crimes. Second, there is the danger that the development of special organizations may create redundancy that will complicate instead of simplifying an effective response to a crisis.

During the various simulations, whether a regular organizational framework or a specialized body was activated, certain patterns of administrative behavior emerged that have serious implications in a siege irrespective of the management orientation of the responding units. The patterns raise small but potentially serious operational problems and also broader issues relating to effective command and control.

At the start of each simulation, as in actual incidents, the character of the initial response was determined largely by the behavior of the first law-enforcement officers to be cognizant of the seizure and the first officers to arrive at the scene.

In evaluating reaction time in all the exercises, it must be noted that the logs kept were of uneven quality, particularly in the earlier simulations, when the techniques were just being refined. The degree of detail in the chronicles often depended on the participants' willingness to employ the recording equipment ordinarily used to monitor police or military radio nets. Some of the initial logs were just outlines of what transpired. A later exercise produced a twenty-page, highly detailed account of a simulation recorded by the Tulsa, Oklahoma, Police Department.

The available information showed certain patterns that are useful not only in exploring the initial administrative reactions in the simulations but also in illustrating the need for sharp responses to hostage-taking incidents.

In all the exercises the responding police departments experienced various problems in communication, which often hindered a quick response to the crisis. The communications problems produced not only errors in judgment but also failures or malfunctions in necessary equipment. In more than one exercise Murphy's Law applied: "If it can go wrong, it will." Members of the response force were always tempted to contend that the defects would not have happened in an actual incident, but most of the participants recognized that they not only would have occurred but also possibly would have been magnified in the pressure of an actual crisis.

In several of the simulations the police took over thirty minutes to arrive at the scene of the incident. Often the delay was because of the slow response of the officer who received the call to notify his superiors quickly. For example, in one simulation the dispatcher failed to report the incident immediately because he thought it was a hoax and because he was busy answering calls about automobile accidents—the simulation was conducted on a day when there were ice storms. While the dispatcher's response was understandable, it illustrates that the unwillingness to accept the crisis coupled with other concerns can lead to the loss of vital time in responding to an incident of terrorism.

A quick reaction was also delayed because of lack of discipline in the use of the radio net. Indeed, in a number of simulations there was confusion because the different forces involved were operating on different channels and consequently could not establish contact with each other. Thus, for example, in one exercise the following events were recorded:

At this time I've not heard anything from 5A1, who was the initial unit sent to the scene of the reported hostage-taking incident. It is now 15 minutes since the first phone call from the hostage holders. Initially Lieutenant ——— was having difficulty getting hold of a dispatcher on Channel 7. Lieutenant ——— is now on route to the . . . where the hostages reportedly are being held. Channel 7 on this radio is not transmitting or receiving. . . . I have checked with the outer perimeter officers; they stated that they are unable to transmit or receive on Channel 7.

The frustration of being unable to evolve a quick and effective initial response to an incident because of communication difficulties and associated problems is aptly expressed in the following statement:

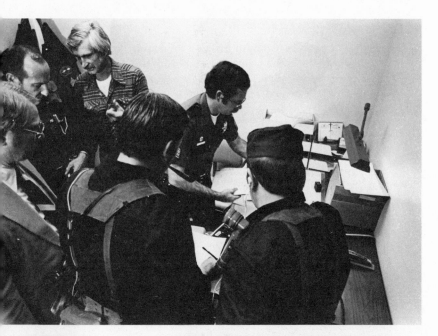

Tension in the command post: the police are also hostages. *Courtesy of Port of Portland, Oregon, Police Department.*

The role I had was that of the Special Operations Team and assisting in communications at the command post. I felt frustrated as communications were inadequate due to faulty equipment, also I was tense not knowing to what extent the negotiations were or not successful.

The problems related to defects in equipment and ineffective procedures continually plagued the responding forces and prevented their taking adequate measures at the start of many of the simulations and ultimately throughout them. The failure to use the radios effectively—even when they were functioning— constantly plagued the operation. As another participant noted:

Communication was poor between the command post and negotiators.

Communication was lax, it seemed that information from the field to the C-P was not quick enough in getting to the people.

The failures in initial communication impeded the development of a rapid response because the responding forces were unable to acquire information from the site of the incident. Communication problems also barred development of a coordinated response from headquarters, the officers in the field, and other concerned personnel. Thus the problems associated with a slow reaction time also prevented the development throughout the simulation of a coordinated administrative organization for effective command, control, and crisis management. The uncertainty of individuals in and outside the command post was both the cause and the result of difficulties in organizing for the siege. The degree of confusion can be seen in the following account written by a participant:

Too much confusion in the command post with little control over the personnel. Needed better assigned positions, and numbers [were] not knowledgeable of a lot of radio call signs to all the personnel involved. . . .

This confusion ultimately complicated the work of the supervisors in the field and the senior commanders in the command post, who were soon faced with the crucial task of bringing a degree of order out of the initial chaos. Two candid remarks aptly illustrate the concerns and challenges of those individuals, one a staff duty officer, the other a chief:

> My first impression of the role in which I found myself was that I had to establish some order and organization in the situation.
>
> However, I felt that my good intentions were not achieved. I was not sure that the orders I issued were carried out. It was extremely difficult to get an accurate assessment of the situation and determine what action had been taken before my arrival.
>
> I also felt a nagging and persistent concern that our simulation would become real. My effectiveness was hampered by my foreknowledge, but I just couldn't delegate responsibility.

The initial responses to the simulated hostage-takings underscored two points. First, even if contingency plans did exist, they often broke down rapidly under the pressure of events. Second, although a degree of organization and control would evolve as the simulation continued, crucial time was lost at the inception of the crisis. This loss of time not only greatly complicated the successive attempts to coordinate a response but also intensified the dangers faced by the hostages during the early phases of the siege.

The lack of coordination that often accompanies the early responses to an incident also bars the development of an effective tactical response. In the long run it not only prevents effective management of the siege but also raises serious policy questions, particularly in relation to the conflicts that can and do occur when the reacting forces are drawn from different jurisdictions. These policy issues are discussed in Chapter 17.

12 Administering under the Gun
The Attempt to Manage the Siege

In all the simulations the initial shock and disorientation created by the assault were replaced by attempts by the responding forces to develop a series of countermeasures at the start of what was—often rightly—forecast as a protracted siege. As the key officials and their staffs met in the command posts that were established, and as the tactical teams were deployed on the perimeter, a degree of routine began slowly to replace the ad hoc reaction that characterized the early responses of the participating police or military units.

To understand the decision-making process that determines the outcome of the simulation, it is essential to discuss the environment in which the participants outside the barricaded area carry out their respective roles. Various environmental factors influence the officials within the command post and on the periphery of the operations center and must be taken into account by the members of any force, from patrol officers to chief, in a protracted siege.

In all the simulations the site used as the command post tended to be too crowded. While the number of people often decreased as responsibilities were delegated and roles were assigned, the operations center still contained many unnecessary personnel throughout the exercises. As a result physical and mental discomfort often interfered with the resolution of the crisis. The combination of the cigarette smoke, the noise level, the heat, and other adverse conditions resulting from overcrowding promoted fatigue, which intensified as the siege continued. The lack of sufficient space to sit or work also diminished physical alertness as the initial energy levels created by the excitement surrounding the event gave way to grudging recognition that the hostage-taking might not be settled quickly by either resort to force or successful negotiations. Of perhaps even greater negative impact was the mental fatigue that accompanied the physical discomfort, which was intensified by the tension within the command center. The overcrowded conditions and the constant movement produced the appearance and, consequently, the feeling among many of the participants that all was not under control. This feeling acted as a barrier to careful planning and execution, which are better done in an atmosphere of relative calm. The need for a workable physical and mental environment was particularly apparent when one considered that the possibilities are intensified for conflict among the participants at all levels because they are working under stress. The command post "is potentially full of conflicting interests and hierarchical problems,"[1] and the tensions are escalated by the bad working conditions. At the same time in most of the simulations many individuals were attracted to the center of the action even if they had no specific function there.

The atmosphere of urgency and the crowded conditions were often particularly detrimental to the performances of key personnel, such as the field commander and the designated hostage negotiators. The field commander could be influenced to make decisions to impress the other personnel in the command post instead of considering objectively the events surrounding the incident. For example, the temptation to take a hard line in front of the "troops" could consciously or unconsciously influence the senior decision maker. The strain was also telling on the negotiators. In a number of instances they may have been more concerned with meeting the expectations of their commander than with developing the necessary empathy to evolve an effective negotiative posture with the terrorists. Therefore, although conditions might call for modification, two basic lessons emerged from the placement of personnel in the command center: (1) the personnel in the command post should be severely limited to key senior officers and their aides, and (2) whenever possible, the negotiators should be in close communication with but kept apart from the officers who ultimately make the decisions.

Throughout all the simulations particular attention was given to evaluating the performance of critical personnel both within and outside the command center. The key personnel were the senior military officer or chief of police and his staff, the tactical team leaders, the press liaison personnel (when appropriate), and the hostage negotiators (the negotiators' performance will be presented in detail in Chapter 14). Since each simulation had a different cast of characters, the relative importance of each role differed, but certain common elements emerged among the decision makers and their crucial staff personnel. Those common elements not only determined how the siege was managed but also raised serious questions about planning, refinement of training techniques, and issues associated with multijurisdictional coordination and cooperation.

The Senior Commander

In all the simulations certain common patterns emerged in the behavior of the most-senior commander involved in the operation. Those observations must, however, be subject to qualification since the command structure differed in each of the simulations: the unique aspects of the hierarchy employed by each responding unit must always be kept in mind.

In only two of the simulations were the persons in direct control the same persons who would be in overall command if a real incident occurred. In the Tulsa, Oklahoma, and the Oklahoma University simulations the chiefs of the respective responding forces directed the operations against the "terrorists."

In another exercise, in Panama, the base commander did not supervise the response, but the senior commander was a lieutenant colonel who might have been in charge of the operation if the situation warranted it. In most of the other exercises the chief of police was frequently present but chose to assume observer status instead of taking command. Consequently, the chain of command for most of the exercises was truncated and therefore not totally realistic. The operations were primarily conducted by field commanders, who were called on to make policy decisions that would, in all probability, be made at a senior level in an actual incident. Even when the chiefs of police did take charge, the decision-making process did not reach the civilian officials (mayors or commissioners) or the military officers (base commanders) who would bear the over-all responsibility for the conduct and the outcome of an actual operation. This defect, while not critical in evaluating the effectiveness of crisis management, will nevertheless be corrected in future simulations, where, it is anticipated, all of the senior police and elected and nonelected civilian officials in the particular jurisdiction will directly experience how it feels to make the critical decisions in the command post.

Irrespective of the rank of the most-senior commanders, they all tended to fail to delegate responsibility. They attempted to command all aspects of the operations in part because, except for the police chiefs, they were primarily field officers. They were ordinarily concerned with tactical coordination in relatively small-scale incidents, not crises of sufficient magnitude to call for the highest level of involvement of the officers and officials. In essence, the commanders in most of the simulations were given responsibilities that they usually would not have handled, and they chose to follow the path of their own experience by treating the crises primarily as problems that could be resolved in the field under their own direction.

Yet the temptation was still there even for the more-senior commanders, who would ordinarily have assumed direct command in a large-scale crisis and who were constantly delegating authority in carrying out their daily functions. Even they would often make decisions that in an actual crisis should ideally be delegated either to the immediate staff or to the field forces. This tendency to take charge in part reflected the willingness of the senior officers to evaluate their own performances in a training exercise. Although this willingness to take the initiative was most impressive, their unwillingness or inability to delegate responsibilities could prevent the development of an effective response in a large-scale crisis. It should be noted, however, that with only one exception the senior officers avoided the dangers involved in attempting to both command the operation and engage in direct negotiations with the terrorists.

Despite the problems associated with delegating responsibility under trying circumstances, all of the designated senior commanders ultimately did assume their roles, and by the midpoint of the simulations they had developed a degree of routine in meeting the ongoing crisis. Yet, even then, it was debatable whether the development of an orderly, organized response resulted from more effective management techniques as the simulations progressed or simply the intuitive establishment of some order once all the participants began to settle down to the siege.

Even when some coordination and delegation of responsibilities did occur, there was often inefficiency in the utilization of staff personnel, particularly in the area of intelligence. In exercise after exercise the senior officers failed both to cull all the information they could from interviews with released hostages or biodata that was planted by the Study Group and available if the proper channels were followed. This particular weakness was less apparent in the military units who participated in various simulations. Since their operational missions as a matter of course emphasized the collection and evaluation of information, they gathered more intelligence during their simulations than the police forces did.

The Tactical Units

Breakdowns were particularly common in communication and coordination between the command post and the tactical units in the field. This was particularly vexing when the tactical units involved in a simulation were drawn from different organizations—both military and civilian. For example, in one exercise that involved both regular police and air-security personnel, there was not an integrated tactical response throughout the simulation. Even when only police units were employed—which would be the case in virtually any actual incident of terrorism—there was often a lack of coordination between the local police and the specialized operations units or tactical teams, who were often called in from other jurisdictions or from the state police. The lack of integration was further aggravated by the different orientations of the regular units and the tactical teams. The latter's action orientation was at times at odds with the negotiating process that usually was taking place at the command post. The lack of integration can readily be seen in the impressions of one of the participants in the Portland, Oregon, simulation:

From the beginning of the exercise it seemed as though civilian authorities completely forgot about the eight military members that had surrounded the building. For some time the civilian men in the command center had open communications with the military but were not kept informed about all the activities that the civilians were doing.

Our personnel in the field had no idea as to what personnel were in the area, nor what position they had.

As another officer aptly noted:

[I] found excess numbers of officers . . . from different departments. Appeared that each was doing his own thing to a degree without any one person in command. Many decisions were being made without coordination with other command officers.

The lack of coordination between the tactical units and the command post and among representatives of different organizations often barred the development of an effective strategy. Coordination of tactical measures and negotiative techniques is essential to achieve the strategic goals of release of the hostages and apprehension of the terrorists.

Confronted with the problems of developing a coordinated response to the seizure of hostages by well-trained and highly motivated terrorists, the commanders and their staffs had to reconcile conflicting demands while the potential for personality clashes within the command post increased. Faced with the task of exercising command and control over the often-diverse tactical units at the perimeter, the senior officers were subject to heightened tensions during the siege. Yet, for all the problems that they experienced, they could not share the more immediate threats and the far more intense feelings experienced by the hostages, whose lives were subject to barter on the other side of the barricade.

13 Life in front of the Gun
Adjusting to Terror

As the personnel assemble in the command post and the tactical units are deployed, some kind of organization starts to replace the shock after the initial seizure. While the field commander and his, or her, staff begin to deal with problems of logistics and coordination, a sense of administrative purposefulness enables the members of the responding forces to develop a necessary detachment from the crisis. They start to evolve a routine, they begin to minister to the terrorist threat, and they begin to adjust.

For the hostages there is no opportunity to develop a sense of detachment based on administrative tacks and professional concerns. They are held captive by terrorists, often masked and nameless, who may view them as little more than bargaining chips in a deadly game. As victims they experience an intimate sense of dread that cannot be shared by those on the other side of the barricade. Yet the hostages, either consciously or unconsciously, begin to make their own adjustments to the fearful environment in which they find themselves. They bring to the situation a degree of mental order that partially replaces the disorientation and shock they felt at the time of capture.

Although in all the simulations the responses of the individual hostages differed as a result of their different personalities, certain patterns nevertheless emerged. Knowledge of the patterns may be important in the long run not only for potential

A dehumanized target is easier to kill. *Courtesy of Tulsa, Oklahoma, Police Department.*

victims of terrorism but also for the responding units who must meet a terrorist threat. Although the hostages' impressions were of necessity subjective, and their experiences took place in a simulation, their observations are a means of appreciating what a hostage feels in an actual incident. Forced to accept the role of hostage, the simulation victims had to live in and adjust to the circumstances in which they found themselves.

For most of the hostages in the exercises the experience of being held captive transcended a routine training exercise. Many of them embarked on voyages of self-discovery that were meaningful long after the simulations were over. By seeing how they responded in a stressful situation, the hostages could learn lessons that went beyond the techniques that many of them employed in their work as police officers, military personnel, and bureaucrats. As the victims accepted their roles, many no longer viewed the simulation objectively as a simple training technique. As one individual aptly noted:

> As a hostage I can see how devastating such an act would be to the average "man on the street." No one—or very few—individuals in this country are prepared for this type of violence. I found it very easy to be caught up in the role playing and to look at the exercise as a real training *experience* [Italics added].

The simulation experience enabled the victims not only to evaluate their responses under stress but also to appreciate how others feel when they face the barrel of a terrorist's gun. As they began adjusting to their captivity, many of them shared the view recorded by a foreign-service officer in one of the earlier exercises: "Even though this was a simulated exercise I believe the emotions and feelings which I experienced are valid and would be operative in a real situation."

With the passage of time each individual started to cope with the crisis in a different way. While there were shared experiences, it is interesting to see the different responses that developed after the initial seizure. There were individuals who from the start accepted that there was little that they could do. Consequently they took an essentially passive role. One hostage candidly noted: "I began to resign myself to the event and decided that the best strategy would be to try not to antagonize my captors. . . . I felt resigned to my fate." That acceptance of the situation was shared by others, who recognized that their survival depended in part on not asserting themselves in any manner. Another hostage staged that he "tried to obey all orders so as not to draw attention to myself." Yet, even with outward acceptance, other hostages devised means by which they might remain alert. One victim sought to keep active in the following manner: "To keep my mind busy, I was making a conscious effort to remember identity details and tie them to the names of the various terrorists." Others went beyond the attempt to keep alert and avoid falling into a dangerous lethargy by developing their own plans. Some of them began devising active responses to the situation. One hostage noted, "Resolved to follow orders and directions; immediately began to formulate escape plans."

It is interesting to see how certain conditions continued to create disorganization and confusion concerning the passage of time, despite the attempts to cope with the crisis. Thus, while one victim maintained that "time passed surprisingly quickly for me," another noted, "The 13 hours I spent as a hostage was much more than I expected." What is most striking about the latter impression is that the simulation in which the hostage participated was of eight hours' duration. Many of the hostages could not develop a sense of time in the narrow universe in which they found themselves.

The confusion was readily apparent when the terrorists placed paper bags and blindfolds on selected victims. The sensory deprivation had the following effect on one of the hostages:

I felt some fear when I was handcuffed and the bag was placed over my head I did not know what was going to happen or how far "these people" would really go.

I began to calm down later after the bag was removed but still felt very uncomfortable and unsure of the situation. The idea of not knowing what would happen was upmost in my mind.

Even with the continual uncertainty, as the simulation progressed, all the hostages increasingly sought to develop their own ways of dealing with the terrorists. Some attempted to establish rapport with their captors, much like people involved in actual situations. One police hostage observed that he "played on the sympathy of Leila [the terrorist]. . . . I observed if you agreed with her cause your chances of survival were better."

Those attempts to reach out and establish a relationship with the terrorists were not without humor and pathos. In one simulation a white hostage—ironically, one who was trained in human relations—attempted to gain the confidence of two black terrorists by telling them, "Some of my best friends are. . . ." The responses of the terrorists are not printable. One won-

A hostage appeals for his life. *Courtesy of the Port of Portland, Oregon, Police Department.*

ders what would have happened to the victim if her remarks had occurred in an actual incident.

Particularly interesting were the exercises in which hostages took a contrasting approach and attempted to assess the dedication of the terrorists by deliberately antagonizing them. Although such a posture would appear to be exceedingly dangerous, the hostages' behavior in the simulations was not at odds with actual situations where hostages chose to take a hard line and often paid the consequences. In three of the exercises there were individuals who could not restrain their anger at being held captive. The following attitudes expressed by a hostage are striking:

I had been designated with the name Hardass and was somewhat shocked when the terrorists taped my legs, and only mine, to the chair.

At the same time, however, I felt relieved because I believed that, should the terrorists need a hostage to waste, they would take someone more readily available that took less work to unsecure.

A dangerous assumption indeed!

In addition to the patterns of individual behavior, interpersonal dynamics started to develop among the hostages as the simulation progressed. On one hand groups such as the following were recorded by one victim: "We as hostages became disassociated from each other. We had a couple of excellent chances to overpower the terrorists, but we did not move as a group." On the other hand, in the same simulation the following occurred, as reported by another hostage:

> As the incident went on, a solidarity developed between some of the hostages. A communication system of touch and eye contact developed, waiting for an opportunity to escape.
> Many of the hostages gave up. Maybe because their hands were tied, but many of them sat without thinking.

Even when a degree of solidarity was achieved, there were often threats of interpersonal conflict among the hostages, who continued to develop their own individual strategies for survival. As the foreign-service officer noted:

> The attempts by the schoolteacher and reservist to alleviate the situation, in my opinion, were selfishly motivated and shallow. I ignored them. . . . There was one thing which momentarily angered me: when ———— volunteered that he had seen my picture in the newspaper as a CIA agent some months before, I was incredulous. I felt that it was totally uncalled for and could have only hurt the group. The comment was, however, in keeping with ————'s character.

The informer, incidentally, was the "hardass" noted earlier.

It was particularly interesting to observe how the relationships between the hostages and the terrorists developed in the later phases of the simulations. None of the simulations lasted long enough to see the emergence of the Stockholm Syndrome, a condition often cited as occurring between captor and captive in prolonged hostage-takings. The term was coined because of the behavior of bank employees who were held hostage in that Danish city. Such behavior is also known as identification with the aggressor, and it involves transference. It includes "strange feelings of camaraderie, closeness, empathy, friendship, even love that often develop between hostages and captives, between victims and victimizers."[1] In the simulations different relationships were established based on the personalities of the individuals in the group and how they interacted. The observations that follow have implications not only for potential victims of an incident but also for those who must respond to such a crisis.

Toward the end of the simulations many of the hostages had an intense feeling of isolation from the world outside. Even when the police were diligently attempting to effect their release, the victims had little knowledge of what was happening outside of the barricade. In many instances the information that was available was often distorted by the terrorists in order to undermine any remaining confidence that the captives had in the performance of the responding forces. It was therefore not unusual for hostages to make statements such as, "I found that I was getting very angry at the cops." In the exercises this lack of trust was often in part the result of ineffectual negotiations, a problem that is evaluated in Chapter 14.

The frustration and anger, as well as the fear, that the hostages experienced throughout the simulations served to underscore that in many ways a hostage's fate is far more uncertain than that of a prisoner, who at least knows when his term is over and at least is protected by some institutional rules within the jail. Even a prisoner of war is in a better position than a hostage. At least a POW has a military code of behavior, a sense of corporate loyalty, and the Geneva Convention, which does exist despite violations. In contrast, there is no code of conduct for hostages and no reason that they should give their lives for the corporation that employs them. In one of the simulations a hostage who had undergone POW training as part of his duties as a pilot cogently brought home the difference between being a hostage and a POW in the following remarks: "There's a unique difference between being a prisoner of war (POW) and a hostage. In all of our POW training we're taught to resist. In a hostage situation there's no thought to offer resistance to the terrorists."[2]

While some of the simulations ended in stalemates, many were "resolved" by the resort to force. The assaults by the police or military units will be evaluated later, but the impact on the hostages often was sobering. They were angered, frustrated, and fatigued, and it took time for many of them to get out of their hostage roles. Even when they did, their experiences would shape their attitudes in the future toward the threat of terrorism. The lessons learned were particularly valuable for those who one day might, by their actions at the other side of the barricade, determine the fate of actual hostages. Perhaps one of the hostages, who in actuality a member of a police force, best expressed the valuable lesson that can be learned by facing the terrorist's gun in a simulation: "As a person, I could put myself in the position of a real hostage, understanding the fear that they fear and could be more sympathetic to a hostage and the taker. This was a great experience and will be helpful in the future as a hostage negotiator." It could also be helpful to the members of the tactical team, the field commander, and all the others who in their positions have the responsibility to meet the potential terrorist threat.

14 You Can't Negotiate by the Numbers

Over the past years a variety of new techniques have been introduced to the law-enforcement community. Some of the methods that have been developed by behavioral scientists and serving police officers involve the training of personnel in hostage negotiation. The initial impetus for the creation and refinement of such programs was based on several interrelated factors. First, as a result of the Munich tragedy of September 5, 1972, police and military forces began to recognize that their tactical options were not sufficient to deal with terrorist threats and that consequently it was imperative that their personnel learn what has been called *hostage management* or *hostage negotiation*. Second, because of a revolution in communications, police forces greatly speeded up their responses to crimes in progress. As a result, it was increasingly common for criminals to seize hostages as they were caught in the act, in order to have a means of negotiating their escape. Finally, "crazies, crusaders, and criminals"[1] often seized victims as a means of dramatizing their causes through the mass media.

The pioneering applications of hostage negotiation can be traced to the special teams organized by Dr. Harvey Schlossberg,[2] a psychologist who became a serving officer in the New York City Police Department. Other police forces were also innovative in providing alternatives to arms in a barricade situa-

Negotiating under the gun.

tion. The British and the Dutch, as a result of protracted sieges, also greatly refined negotiative skills.

From those early efforts the techniques of negotiation have been disseminated to the state and local levels all over the United States. A wide variety of courses have been conducted for the police officers who have been designated as negotiators for their departments. The proliferation of training programs of uneven quality by both public officials and private consultants has underscored the trendy aspect that the techniques have in contemporary police science. Many agencies, from large urban departments to small county sheriff's offices, now have personnel who, for better or worse, have undergone at least rudimentary training.

The proliferation of negotiation courses has been accompanied by a proliferation of books and articles on the subject. Just as emphasis earlier was placed on providing training and material in the tactical aspects of a hostage situation, hostage management now is a popular area of concern. The relatively recent origins of both approaches demonstrate how the law-enforcement community attempts to meet the threat of terrorism and also raises questions about the lack of integration in applying both approaches in actual incidents.

While there have been excellent innovations in negotiative skills, it is essential to note three interrelated problem areas: the development and refinement of the methodology of negotiation, the training employed, and the outcome in an actual incident. Problems in those areas influenced the performance of the police and the military units in all the simulations and raised serious questions about their capacity to utilize the techniques effectively when an incident occurs.

Despite advances in the development of systematic negotiative skills, hostage negotiation is still not a science but an imperfect art. By relating psychological assumptions with operational concerns from past experience, a series of principles has been refined that form the core of any negotiation strategy. The conventional wisdom dictates, for example, that the negotiator should always stall for time, that something should not be given away for nothing, and that there may be common patterns of behavior based on a classification of hostage-takers' differing psychological states.[3] While those assumptions have some validity, it is unfortunate that in many instances they are presented to law-enforcement personnel in a checklist format: the series of possibilities can be a helpful guide in developing a response, but the list is often taken too literally by those who must negotiate.

The checklist approach can be seen not only in the literature but also in many training programs. While a variety of administrative measures unquestionably must be taken into account in preparing for an incident, the user of the checklist starts to falter when he or she attempts to understand and deal with behavior under stress. It is one thing to note the need to set up perimeters, control communications with the hostage-takers, and provide for press liaison officers. Those procedures are always valid and can be made operational. It is quite another thing to attempt to provide behavioral keys that can be employed by the negotiator in the attempt to resolve an incident. It is not that the keys are not helpful, it is just that they are often presented too literally to those who are undergoing training.

Delivering the ransom: there will be no hidden weapons. *Courtesy of the Port of Portland, Oregon, Police Department.*

Perhaps even more disturbing is the way that the checklist type of training tends to encourage a procedural response to the complex behavior that is present in any hostage-taking incident. Most of the training provides techniques by the numbers instead of a means by which negotiators can appreciate the crucial dynamics accompanying an actual incident. A simulation provides a setting where the negotiator starts to appreciate that one cannot resolve a crisis by the numbers. Yet, as we shall see, in all of the simulations some negotiators attempted to employ a rigid response based on the assumptions that had been codified in their training.

Even when effective training is available, the selection of negotiators all too often is not based on the psychological attributes and experience that can aid an individual in becoming an effective practitioner, but on such unrelated factors as the person's availability for training, his or her ability to get the assignment, and the temptation to undergo a course to punch another number that may promote career development. A diploma or certification in hostage negotiation does not guarantee that a person is qualified to deal with a threat, and it may even provide a false sense of knowledge—which, when imperfectly applied, does more harm than good. Even good training will have no meaning if the negotiator lacks the sensitivity to listen to the person on the other end of the telephone line or to develop empathy with what is being said. Indeed, the case can be made that an experienced police officer with no formal training may do far better in dealing with a hostage-taking than an immature or authoritarian officer who cannot develop effective human-relations techniques.

The Simulation Experience

In the simulations the level of training varied greatly among the designated negotiators. While some had basic training, others assumed the negotiator role with only limited readings in the subject. Some of the negotiators had not been subject to any preparation at all for their assignment. A few officers had negotiated intuitively over a wide variety of issues during their extensive field experience, but most of the participants, even if they had training, had never had an opportunity to test their techniques in a realistic setting. For many of them the simulation was their baptism under fire.

It is not the intent of this chapter to analyze in detail how the negotiators performed in their new roles, but rather to indicate certain problems that have emerged. The simulations had implications in terms of the techniques of negotiation, the type of training that is now being employed, the recruitment of potential negotiators, and the need for further refinement of method in this still-popular field of concern.

The Negotiation Guidelines

In each of the simulations the responding forces varied in terms of the preparation and scope of the guidelines that they employed in hostage negotiations. In some of the exercises the police had not even developed the most cursory policies to be utilized, while in others there were clearly stated procedures that, ideally, would be relied on in the event of an incident.

Despite this diversity, most of the responding forces developed their directives on the basis of commonly accepted techniques that have been presented in a wide variety of negotiation training courses. The plethora of published material on negotiation guidelines will not be repeated here. Rather, certain key assumptions that were incorporated into the operations orders of the responding units will be presented in order to illustrate how they were employed in the different simulations. The following evaluation may underscore some defects in the negotiations that became apparent in the exercises and could impede departments in successfully resolving an incident without resort to force.

In all of the simulations the responding units did have a negotiation team ready to assume its duties. In only one simulation were provisions made for additional teams to be ready to take over if the siege became protracted or if the initial negotiators were unable to carry out their duties effectively. A further complication was that field commanders were often unwilling to change the team even when it became obvious that a negotiator could not communicate effectively with the terrorists. This lack of flexibility may have been in part a product of bureaucratic inertia: the commanders, having established a necessary routine, were unwilling to make necessary changes until the credibility of a negotiator had been so totally destroyed that the need to change personnel was urgent.

In all but one of the simulations it was assumed that the negotiator should not be empowered to make final decisions. In that one exceptional exercise the military commander was negotiating effectively, but unfortunately he permitted his tactical commander to assault the terrorist position at his own discretion. The results were disastrous to the hostages. Even when the negotiator was not a senior commander, the officer in charge was often tempted to participate indirectly in the negotiating. Although the commanders did not talk to the terrorists, in many instances they attempted to advise the negotiator so closely that the latter could not take the initiatives necessary to establish rapport with the hostage-takers. Necessary exchanges were thwarted by the negotiator's tendency to ask for confirmation by his superior of any request. Concomitantly, the senior officer would disrupt the development of a routine by constantly interfering in conversations between the hostage-takers and negotiators to offer advice. Such interference led to disjointed discussions instead of a guarded dialogue between the negotiator and the perpetrator. The same unwillingness to delegate authority often prevented the senior officer from effectively coordinating the activities of the various personnel and units involved in the exercises.

It was particularly striking in all of the simulations that the negotiators and their commanders tended to interpret literally the guideline that is constantly employed in training courses: "Never give up anything without receiving something in return." The negotiators and their superiors often refused to make even symbolic gestures that might encourage good faith and successful negotiations. Thus there were occasions when it would have been advisable for the police to give the perpetrators some water or food without demanding something in return, in order to indicate their willingness to engage in serious negotiations. The delivery of small amounts of food and water does not enable the captors to achieve any self-sufficiency and indeed may make them more acutely aware that the authorities ultimately control the environment. Consciously or unconsciously, terrorists must be made to recognize that they are dependent on the decisions of the people on the other side of the barricade. Perhaps even more important, such a gesture serves to indicate to the hostages that they have not been abandoned by the people "on the outside."

This unwillingness to be flexible was often carried to dangerous extremes. For example, in exercise after exercise demands for food and water—which were needed not only by the terrorists but also by the hostages—were met only very late in the sieges and only when a give-and-take was evident. The resulting short-term victory for the negotiators often entailed a long-term loss. In the latter phases of many of the exercises a hostage might be released in exchange for hamburgers, but by that time irreparable harm had already been done to the potential for successful negotiations. In too many instances the terrorists and negotiators were polarized, the police did not employ the exchange as a means of acquiring intelligence during the exchange, and the degree of animosity that developed led to a final assault, in which many of the hostages were killed.

This inability or unwillingness on the part of the negotiators to "give something for nothing" raised a number of serious questions about the training that potential negotiators receive. Because the negotiations took place in a simulation, however realistic, negotiators could play a game that might have been impossible in an actual incident. At the initiation of all of the exercises the terrorists intentionally avoided precipitous actions, such as killing most of the hostages, in order not to force the police to respond with an assault. Such a limitation was written into the script because one of the prime goals of the simulations was to provide a setting in which negotiators could develop and practice their skills in an extended siege. In future simulations, in order to place more pressure on the negotiators and lessen their tendency to game, more dramatic and drastic actions may be taken at the initiation of the attacks in order to force the negotiators more effectively into their roles. In the second simulation with the 51st Security Group in Osan, Korea, the terrorists intentionally murdered a hostage at the inception of the exercise. This overt act not only underscored the seriousness of the situation but also raised questions concerning the commonly held assumption that, if a hostage is killed, the tactical approach should be employed as quickly as possible.[4]

The negotiators lacked flexibility in the simulations not only because of the severe limitations placed on their initiatives by operations commanders but also because of their socialization into the law-enforcement profession. Many of the negotiators were used to giving orders and expected them to be obeyed. They had difficulty changing their roles and mentally taking off their uniforms. For some of the policemen it was difficult to carry out discussions with individuals who were engaging in criminal acts. This difficulty was amplified because the officers were expected not only to communicate but also to negotiate with the perpetrators. In many instances the hostage negotiators found themselves unable as police officers to negotiate because they interpreted any concessions on their part as signs of weakness instead of recognizing that concessions were essential in any successful negotiation.

The rigidity also carried over to the conversations recorded in the simulations. In too many instances the negotiators did not listen to what was being said at the other end of the telephone line. They tended to give orders instead of attempting to understand the demands and underlying motivations of the terrorists. Consequently, despite the dictum that the negotiator should "assess the motivation of the perpetrator,"[5] many of the individuals who played the role were too busy making demands instead of analyzing the mental state of the perpetrators.

This lack of sensitivity was particularly apparent in the inability of the negotiators to begin to empathize with the terrorists. Their unwillingness to share the feelings of the people on the other side of the barricade reflected in part the attitude that empathy and identity were one and the same. As a result officers were often unable to get into the frame of mind of the terrorists because they feared that the necessary introspection might not only lead them to be viewed as weak by their superiors but also subject them to their own form of the Stockholm Syndrome described in Chapter 13.

This behavior not only acts as a barrier to effective negotiation but also severely limits the negotiators' ability to acquire vital information about the condition of both the hostages and the terrorists. Such information can be useful in developing a response strategy based on sufficient intelligence data. By not listening the negotiators did not learn.

The reliance on doing things by the numbers and the lack of sufficient sensitivity for effective negotiation point to two defects in current negotiation training. First, the emphasis on technique at the cost of developing awareness often fails to break down the potential negotiator's authoritarian manner, which may be necessary on patrol but often is a detriment in the personal interaction necessary for effective negotiation. Second, the training is not realistic since it does not offer a setting in which people are actually forced to develop the necessary human-relations skills. Learning to negotiate by the numbers in a classroom environment is not enough.

Through the simulation technique the negotiators started to appreciate that a reliance on procedure is not enough when duties must be carried out in a real setting under pressure. One of the participants expressed the emotions he experienced, emotions that would not have developed in a classroom setting or an exercise in academic gaming:

> I felt overwhelmed and at first inadequate until the situation began to settle in a groove. . . . As the anxiety left it was soon replaced by hunger, fatigue—which made the situation seem a little more frustrating.
>
> I felt as though the situation was turning into reality. . . . Near the end the situation began to feel very real and a strong sense of urgency among the team began to develop.

In addition, some negotiators did learn the value of listening instead of giving orders. One of them observed:

> I learned that a negotiator must really try to keep his word if he tells the terrorists that he will try to do something for them.
>
> I felt that the terrorists really wanted to be heard and that to just listen to them would help establish rapport with them.

I learned that the need to gather information about them and to be able to know something about them and their cause would really help.

Perhaps, in the final analysis, the following impression most aptly sums up what the simulations can do for potential negotiators: "I learned that there was much more than just talking to someone on the other end of the phone."

Concluding Observations

In all of the simulations certain characteristics marked the behavior of the negotiators. Those behavior patterns have implications for the selection and performance of the individuals who in the future may have to take on the role of "good broker" under the most stressful circumstances. The effectiveness of the negotiators was often less the result of the training that they had acquired than their own personalities and experiences.

There was no way to predict the performance of the negotiators in the exercises. In part this was because the responding departments decided who would take on the role, and the judgment was not made solely on the basis of past experience or training. In some instances the choice was based largely on the availability of personnel and on other criteria that have no relationship to effective negotiation. The selection process, however, did not necessarily differ from what might transpire in an actual incident. Since none of the police and military units in the simulations had specialized negotiation squads, such as that of the New York Police, they had to make on-the-scene judgments at the inception of an incident. As a result of the simulations a more concerted effort was made to train personnel systematically in negotiation techniques.

There was no correlation between the age and experience of the negotiators and their level of performance. In some instances relatively youthful officers proved to be more effective than purportedly "street-wise" veterans; in other exercises, the opposite held true. Yet there were a few attributes that marked the officers who were successful in negotiation. A number of those attributes appear to be related to simple common sense, but without them it is doubtful that an individual can be an effective negotiator even if he receives extensive training.

The successful negotiator quickly displays a capacity to listen instead of a tendency to control the conversation. Moreover, he can block out the surrounding noise and the conflicting advice that he often receives in the command post in order to concentrate on communicating effectively with the terrorists. In developing the communication, the more effective negotiators are also manifestly able to relate to the perpetrators in a non-threatening manner. That skill is further enhanced by the ability that some have to establish by their voice level an atmosphere of calm both inside the command post and with the terrorists. It is also interesting to note that the most successful are even able to lessen tension by introducing an element of humor in the discussions, in part because of their ability not to take themselves too seriously. Finally, the successful negotiators often are able to establish a routine, which greatly assists in tension reduction. The establishment of a routine in part requires that the concept of time not be introduced into the discussions and acceptance on the part of the participants that the negotiations may extend over a very long period.

Those attributes are derived from impressionistic observations. By themselves they do not constitute the basic requisites for a successful negotiator. Nonetheless, reliance on a checklist or negotiating by the numbers is no substitute for the ability of the negotiator—irrespective of his level of training—to combine patience, compassion, self-discipline, and flexibility—qualities that are often missing in those who define their role in law enforcement in terms of self-assertion, an action orientation, and an inability to listen. Although procedure is certainly crucial in evolving an effective administrative and tactical response to a hostage-taking, a mechanistic approach in short courses or seminars cannot teach human relations by rote.

15 Police-Press Relations

Constitutional Issues Cannot Be Discussed at the Barricade

Because terrorism is a form of theater, the media are important in determining the impact of the act of violence on the public. The treatment accorded to a specific incident can be viewed as a review since the coverage given to a hostage-taking or a bombing may well determine if there will be an audience that will listen to the demands of the terrorists. This does not mean that the media by themselves necessarily cause or encourage acts of terrorism. While at times members of the press have acted in an irresponsible manner, other groups, including the responding authorities, also at times have overreacted and consequently given the terrorists a stage on which they could justify their actions to the public.

Confronted with this reality, both print and electronic journalists must continually attempt to reconcile the pressures from their profession to obtain the story and the public's right to be informed with the equally vital responsibility not to give terrorists a podium from which they can attempt to legitimize their actions. The problem of reconciliation has raised particularly vexing questions in liberal Democratic states, where authorities have often viewed the press as acting irresponsibly and the press, for its part, has contended that suggested limitations in reporting come perilously close to censorship. As a result of those concerns attempts have been made to establish at least informal guidelines that can be used by the media in covering an incident. As is true of any procedural suggestions, the most effective written program may break down under the press of events. Thus the guidelines may be only as good as the willingness of a senior editor to withhold a story at the risk of being scooped by a young stringer from another paper trying to make a quick reputation by covering the story.[1]

Because of the complexity of the media's role in covering an incident, there was an attempt to involve the press in some of the simulations. The object of this involvement was not to explore complex constitutional issues or to test any existing guidelines. Rather, the simulations were a setting in which the media and the law-enforcement community—despite their often inherently adverse roles—could begin to appreciate the special problems that they each might face during an incident.

The observers viewing the assault on television cannot remain detached from the act of terrorism.

In various simulations students played the role of journalists, but whenever possible media professionals were involved in the exercises. Except for designated members of the media who filmed the incidents for future presentation and training purposes, the professional reporters on the scene were expected to cover the story as an actual event. In order to test police-press relations, it was important that the reporters assigned to the story cover it as a fast-breaking crisis.

The levels of realism that were achieved as the press covered the events are aptly illustrated in the following account of one of the earliest simulations: "Such a realistic atmosphere prevailed over the exercise that authentic members of the press were forced to remain behind barricades in a nearby hanger for more than an hour to protect them from possible sniper fire and were threatened with arrest if they left the hanger."[2] The realism could and did strain the relationships between the police and reporters at times, witness the threat of arrest. The exercises were, indeed, a realistic setting in which designated media liaison officers could appreciate the difficulties that they would encounter in working with the media during an actual incident.

At times the tension led to more excessive behavior, for instance, when reporters chose to provide a forum for the hostage-takers in exchange for obtaining an exclusive story. Thus in one instance, where seminar students played media representatives, the following took place:

A writer and photographer from *Newsweek* ran to the All Seasons Arena, secured the terrorists' telephone number from Northern State Power Co., and called them.

Then, after yelling from the middle of the street for a notebook, the photographer broke away from the SWAT team and approached the besieged building. The terrorists were immediately advised to consider him another hostage.[3]

As a result of the growing tension between the media and the press, the "photographer from *Newsweek* magazine was wrestled to the ground . . . [by] an area Special Weapons and Tactics (SWAT) team."[4] One wonders what would have happened if the reporters had been real and the event were covered nationally.

The participation of the media was meant not only to assist authorities in evaluating their capacity to work with the media but also to sensitize the press to how it would feel if they were involved in an actual incident. Whenever possible, reporters were held captive, in order to let them experience what others feel.

The subjective aspects of covering a story as a participant are aptly illustrated by the following impressions of a reporter who was held hostage in one of the simulations.

Anchor: What is it like, what did you feel?

Reporter: Well, I'm not exactly sure what I'm feeling now. I do know that I was scared and I know that I got mad at a lot of things that happened last night and I do also know, if you or anyone is ever going to be a hostage, hope that the police that are trying to help you are well trained. . . . And at the end, when you're sitting in the dark and you're being covered with flashlights and nobody can see what's happening, all of a sudden we heard someone yell out, "Kill them all," and they came roaring into the room, top speed, and the next thing we knew some of the guns started going off and we were wondering, "What if one of them isn't blank?"[5]

While such an experience may not by itself lessen the competition among reporters to get the story, it may prevent members of the media from viewing the hostages in an actual incident of terrorism as nothing more than people without faces, whose uncertain fate may interfere with meeting an evening deadline.

Sometimes police lack the ability to deal effectively with media representatives who are legitimately in pursuit of their stories. The strains that emerge are better experienced in an exercise than in a real incident, where miscalculations can prove fatal. Willingness to profit from a simulation is cogently expressed by the following remarks of a press liaison officer, who compared his experiences in the simulation and in an actual incident:

My reaction to the simulation was much like my reactions to the two extortion bomb threats which we have experienced in the past nine months. . . . When you use your skills and equipment to the utmost of their effectiveness and allow the scenario to unfold, it is then that you learn about your strengths and weaknesses. . . . and this is the objective of an exercise of this type.

That view was mirrored by the account of an aviation information specialist at the same airport, who compared the simulation with a real incident:

I felt much more prepared for the real incident. I knew what I was supposed to do and I went about it. I know this sounds questionable, but it's true. The reality of the situation—as opposed to the unreality of the simulation—never really struck in any significant way. I was just glad I'd been able to botch up in the simulation.

Thus the simulations can at least provide an effective means to prepare the police to work with the press. The press, for their part, are made more sensitive to the complexities that surround an incident. The exercises cannot deal directly with the grave constitutional issues that surround the responsibilities of the media in covering terrorist incidents, but they aptly demonstrate potential problem areas that surface during a crisis, when no one can afford the luxury of a leisurely discussion of legal norms, and when the most sophisticated lawyer's opinion will mean nothing on either side of the barricade.

16 Patterns of Miscalculation That Can Prove Fatal

While the dynamics of each of the simulations was unique, certain patterns emerged that were common to all of the exercises. Those patterns suggest problems that might confront both police and military units as they responded to an incident of terrorism involving the seizure of hostages. The patterns also illustrate difficulties that may occur in any barricade situation; for example, when a robber is caught in the act and seizes captives.

The same problems developed in all of the simulations and should be considered by police and military forces when they train for or experience an incident. In presenting the patterns a chronological approach will be employed, tracing and discussing the difficulties experienced during the various simulations. This account is both a review of "the theater of the obscene" and an evaluation of potential problems to assist authorities in minimizing common difficulties, difficulties that may spell the difference between the successful resolution of an incident and a Munichlike tragedy.

Confusion at the Outset

At the inception of some incidents, even when the dispatcher knew that a drill was to take place, he was often unwilling to accept that an incident had been initiated. Sometimes the first officer notified chose to view the threatening call from the terrorist as a hoax. Such cynicism, while understandable, nevertheless points to an initial barrier to responding to an incident. Since terrorism is often viewed as something that happens to other people in other places, it may be difficult for the officer to accept that the threat of terrorism has become a reality that affects him individually and affects his community collectively. The expression "You have to be kidding" characterizes the inability of even trained officers to accept that an act of terrorism is not merely something to be read about or an abstraction.

Unwillingness to accept that an incident can occur may be particularly prevalent among the personnel of smaller rural police forces, who tend to think that there are no potential targets in their jurisdictions. Their lack of concern probably is more valid than that of police in large urban areas and in localities where there are sensitive targets, but it is important for senior personnel to convey the message that there are no safe havens. Getting this message across without overstating the threat is important if all officers are to take their training programs seriously and not express disbelief in an actual incident, such as a hostage-taking, where disbelief can delay a quick response.

Unwillingness to accept that an incident is actually occurring promoted disorganization in the responding forces at the beginning of the simulations. Since most of the responding forces did not anticipate an actual incident in their areas, the appearance of armed and dedicated revolutionaries often strained the participating units' capacity to organize an administratively sound program to deal with the crisis. Even if the police force had prepared contingency plans—which was more likely among the military police forces—the plans were often ignored or violated because they had not been tested in realistic exercises. The initial confusion in all the simulations was based in part on the need to acquire more information concerning the act, but all too often the quest for more information, however understandable, delayed development of a quick response strategy.

In evaluation after evaluation observers voiced the view that the delays resulted from (1) an absence of prior planning, (2) lack of evaluation techniques to test the plans in action, (3) un-

A study in black and white: a high-visibility target.

willingness to accept that a crisis had started, and (4) a view that "the department is not used to dealing with such incidents—besides, they would not happen here." The early administrative disorientation was particularly apparent when the simulation involved senior commanders or more than one police or military unit. In the former case, as the chain of command went up the ladder, more people became involved in the decision-making process, and the possibilities for problems in coordination and control would surface. Even in simulations where the key decision makers were primarily at the field level, early disorganization tended to be the rule and not the exception. In the latter case the possibilities for administrative immobilization were particularly apparent if the responding force did not quickly establish a liaison with other concerned parties. There was a tendency for each agency or support service to "do its own thing" at the expense of developing an integrated approach to counter the challenge. For example, it was not unusual to see special-weapons-and-tactics teams or bomb-disposal squads from different jurisdictions working at cross-purposes at the inception of an incident. Lack of integration did not pose such a serious problem when the simulations involved military units on installations. Such an environment is easier to control because a perimeter can be established more easily and because the chain of command is clearer with over-all control vested in the base commander. Nevertheless, jurisdictional immobility always made coherent crisis management more difficult, whether the simulation took place in the relatively sanitized environment of an installation or a far-more-complex setting, such as a city street or a public terminal. The problems of potential jurisdictional responses at the local, state, and national level will be discussed in Chapter 17.

The disorganization at the inception of a simulation was intensified by difficulties in communication, both technical and human. In all the simulations, even when prior arrangements were made for telephones between the hostage-takers and the police, there were mechanical breakdowns, which impaired the ability of the police to initiate negotiations. Murphy's Law was again evident in malfunctioning field telephones, busy signals on the only available telephone, and the lack of portable equipment as an alternative means of communication. Even climatic conditions on at least two occasions thwarted rapid contact between police and terrorists. In both cases an electric bullhorn proved useless because the wind carried the voice of the negotiator away from where the hostages were seized. The dangers involved in defective technical communication were heightened in a case where the local telephone company and the police had not developed contingency plans to provide for portable or alternative communications in the event that regular telephone services were defective or nonexistent. In the majority of the simulations prior arrangements had not been able to obtain support from the local telephone company in the event of a prob-

The tactical solution.

Guarding the inner perimeter.

lem. Attempting to call Ma Bell for assistance at the inception of a simulation has an element of gallows humor, but such humor might prove fatal to a victim of a real incident. The need for contingency planning in this area may be obvious, but it has not always been practiced.

Associated technical problems in communication were apparent even after the negotiators or the officers arriving first were able to establish contact with the hostage-takers. In two exercises, where recording devices were attached to the telephone to monitor the conversations, the equipment did not work, thereby limiting the negotiators' ability to acquire the information to carry out their duties. In both cases the equipment in question had not been periodically tested.

The problems of developing and maintaining communication were further aggravated when the negotiators failed to observe the cardinal rule of controlling all communication with the hostage-takers. In one instance a critical discussion was aborted because an unknown third party used the only extension available and thus created a busy signal on the only available phone. Perhaps even more ominous was the ease with which the terrorists in some of the simulations contacted the press to get their demands known, and, conversely, ease with which the individuals who played the role of journalists contacted the terrorists to get the story. The need to control communication may be obvious, but it was violated in several of the exercises.

Ironically, in all the simulations there was a contrasting problem, which often crippled the police in responding throughout the crises: the problem of overcommunication. In all of the exercises there was a lack of radio and telephone discipline on the part of the responding forces. This was particularly the case with the civilian forces, whose personnel were not as well drilled in effective radio or telephone procedures as their military counterparts.

While the availability of hand-held radios has certainly aided police and military forces in carrying out their duties, radios were often counterproductive in the simulations. In all of the exercises it was only by trial and error that a command net was established. Too often one saw the spectacle of responding personnel attempting to contact other parties on a number of different channels. A virtual tower of electronic babel often resulted. The problem was intensified in multijurisdictional exercises, where the responding forces were on different channels. A related phenomenon was the apparent compulsion of many officers to use their radios simply because they were equipped with them. Evidently, "getting on the horn" enabled personnel to feel that they were involved in resolving the crisis. The difficulty was that, while a sense of purpose may have been promoted, it led all too often to confusion, which detracted from the development of a coordinated program to deal with the crisis. From the exercises it is apparent not only that all equipment must be carefully checked and contingency plans drawn up to provide back up equipment but also that the danger of overcommunication through lack of radio discipline must be eliminated.

In some exercises the question of developing communications became part of the bargaining process with potentially disasterous results. Although common sense dictates that it is important to develop communications with the hostage-takers as quickly as possible to initiate the negotiation process, there was a temptation to dismiss this obvious concern at the start of the simulations. Where there was an absence of telephones or a breakdown in equipment, the commanding officers and negotiators often attempted to make the availability of telephones a part of the negotiation process. In two cases the police refused to provide the means of communication unless hostages were released. The result was increased anger on the part of the captors, increased fear on the part of the captives, and a serious delay in initiating the kind of contact that is essential for successful negotiations. The reasons for the delay may relate solely to those simulations, but they confirm a broader problem in negotiations, which is discussed in Chapter 14: the tendency of negotiators to interpret too literally the guideline "Don't give anything away without obtaining a concession."

Often the disorganization at the inception of the simulations was aggravated by physical aspects of the areas designated as the command posts. The layouts of the command centers varied, as a result of the facilities available in the different locales, from rather rudimentary operations areas to more permanent headquarters. Certain environmental factors and associated individual and group reactions always detracted from the management of the sieges.

It was certainly understandable that very impromptu arrangements had to be made at the inception of the incidents, but little attention was given to developing alternative arrangements that could provide the necessary space, equipment, and comfort to enable authorities to deal with a potentially long siege. Except where a regular command center or an adequate alternative facility was available, most of the command posts lacked the requisites to deal with a protracted crisis. The temporary command posts often became permanent, either because it was assumed that the seizure would shortly be resolved or because the importance of an adequate center was not recognized in the first place. The oversight not only could create serious difficulties in a long-term incident but also created conditions that intensified and added to the disorganization accompanying the early responses in the simulations.

Administrative disorganization was often intensified because the command post was too small, not adequately ventilated, and had a high noise level. The discomfort in such an environment made it difficult for the senior personnel and the negotiators to function effectively. The on-site commanders, their staffs, and the hostage negotiators were particularly affected. Just when an atmosphere of purposeful organization was vital, the setting of the command center tended to play up the disorganization that had developed at the start of the crisis. An atmosphere of hectic, purposeless activity was created by the physical setting in which the key decisions were made. While the discomfort may not have affected key personnel at the early stages of the crises, the cumulative effect was significant as the exercises progressed, and it would certainly have become more significant if the simulations had extended well beyond eight hours. It is therefore important to recognize that a temporary command post may prove inadequate if a long-term incident develops and that contingency plans should be made either to improve the temporary command post or to move to a better facility as soon as is practical without disturbing on-going operations.

The discomfort and attendant disorganization was not caused solely by the physical features of the command posts. The physical problems were aggravated in all of the simulations because, without exception, there were too many personnel in the centers throughout the exercises. Some of the unnecessary personnel were present at the start of the simulations because tasks were yet to be delegated to members of the responding force or forces. At the same time another factor came into play: at the start of the crisis unnecessary personnel often stayed at the post because they were not assigned other functions or simply because they wished to be where the action was.

In exercise after exercise, even when there were relatively few individuals participating, the senior field commander was forced to operate from overcrowded facilities. The appearance of unnecessary officers often led to confusion about the delegation of responsibilities, and the ready availability of radios, instead of providing necessary information, often tended to confuse the development of a coherent response, since messages were often fragmented and not presented to the on-site commander in a coherent manner. While this initial disarray lessened as the simulations progressed, the early disorganization in the command posts militated against the rapid development of coordinated responses to the crises. Even in the most complex incident it is essential that those in charge of crisis management be afforded the opportunity to develop their approaches and to work in relative calm. If the noise level, for example, is so loud that "you cannot hear yourself think," how can you manage a crisis?

The individuals designated as hostage negotiators were affected particularly adversely by the discomfort within the command centers. At the very time when it was vital that the negotiators listen carefully to the demands of the hostage-takers, they were often placed in an exceedingly noisy atmosphere, where it was difficult to hear even the voice of the person next to them, much less the terrorist's voice, which often came over a bad telephone connection. This inability to hear not only thwarted the negotiators' attempts to acquire essential information and to start the negotiation process but also added to the strains that they experienced in executing their duties. The prospect of attempting to resolve a potentially dangerous incident in the midst of confusion drained the capacity of the negotiation teams at the inception of the crises and became more aggravated as the sieges went on.

Besides the environmental conditions, the negotiator's capabilities were often lessened by psychological factors because of his placement within the command post. In all but one simulation the negotiator sat right next to the officer in charge of the operation, who was either a shift sergeant or the chief of police. Although proximity was certainly essential in establishing an effective liaison between them, such proximity often placed an added strain on the negotiator, particularly if he was a lower-ranking officer in the responding forces. In a number of instances the negotiator faced the considerable added tension of having to look good in front of his superior officer. It was not clear at times whether the negotiator was attempting to develop a dialogue with the hostage-taker that could resolve the issue or attempting to meet what he thought to be his commander's expectations. The temptation, for example, to act tough in negotiations at times was based not on a particular negotiation technique but on the attitude of the senior commander, who often stood literally right behind the negotiator through much of the simulation. An attempt was made to solve this problem in one exercise by placing the negotiation team either away from the senior crisis-management team or in a separate room. Such an arrangement could add problems because of the need for additional communication links between the two groups. Nevertheless, the negotiators should be placed where they can have ready access to the crisis-management team without feeling the brass sitting in judgment on their every move and where they can engage in vital conversation without contending with a crowd.

In all of the simulations it became increasingly clear that more concern should have been given to providing, within limits, a comfortable working environment for the crisis-management team, the negotiators, and the other personnel who must man the command center. While the discomfort may be ignored initially because of the drama at the outset of an incident, a lack of proper facilities, including such basics as work space, seating, and conference areas, will leave its mark as a siege continues. Little things can mean a great deal as the excitement that characterizes the start of a hostage-taking is replaced by the fatigue and boredom accompanying a crisis that may last days and possibly weeks.

Establishing a Routine

In all of the simulations, either because of concerted planning by the participants or simply because sufficient time had passed, a routine was established by all of the responding units. In part this represented the mirror image of what often happened at the other side of the barricade, where both terrorists and hostages developed their own predictable behaviors after the initial confusion and fear that accompanied the seizure. The patterns that often emerged among the responding units should be instructive to those who may one day be confronted with an actual incident.

As the respective sieges continued, the level of coordination improved between the command post and the tactical units on the perimeter. The initial hectic activity of stationing personnel and securing the area was replaced by attempts to develop plans for the employment of the tactical units in the event that an assault became necessary. The levels of coordination varied with the degree of command and control exercised over the assault forces. When the responding forces had relatively highly trained tactical units, the tactical commanders were often given great latitude to initiate a response if they felt conditions warranted a full assault. By contrast, where the tactical training was minimal, less freedom of action was given to the leaders of the tactical teams. Both approaches did recognize that the degree of permissible independent action in part was dependent on the sophistication and training of the field forces. Unfortunately, while there was a recognition of this between the commanders of the operations and their own assault units, cooperation often broke down when outside tactical units were also brought into play. In one instance, where a military security force was made available to assist the local police on a military installation, and in a second instance, where a state SWAT unit assisted the local police, there was virtually no coordination among the different forces. The field commanders may have been tempted to use the outside force in a secondary role to their own units in part because of a concern about unit cohesion. The result often was inefficient use of all the tactical forces that were available during the simulations. This experience underscores the need for various departments to develop contingency plans and to test the capacities of different tactical units to work as a team in the event of a crisis.

The lack of coordination among tactical teams had an interesting counterpart in the relationship between the tactical unit or units and the negotiators. All too often there was a distinct absence of communication between the negotiators in the command post and the assault units in the field. In part the gap was understandable, given the different responsibilities that each had, but the lack of coordination may represent a potentially dangerous dichotomy between the two. In many of the simulations the negotiators were perceived to be weak sisters, while the negotiators, for their part, felt that the tactical members only thought with their weapons. The difference in perceived attitudes in both parties could make it impossible for all of the units of the responding forces to act as a team. It is therefore suggested that, although it may not be necessary for negotiators and tactical team members to be cross-trained in each other's specialties, they should be members of a single unit and they should develop by constant contact and training an appreciation of each other's problems. The spectacle of negotiators looking down at members of the tactical team in the midst of a simulation raises serious questions about how the unity of the entire department can be maintained if specialized personnel go at cross-purposes.

In all of the exercises there were patterns in the strategies of negotiation and in the negotiators' performance that suggested potential problems in preparing for and responding to an actual hostage-taking. The use of the simulation technique to test negotiative skills was a central purpose in all the exercises. The general observations that follow underscore the importance placed on training negotiators and evaluating them in all of the programs.

In all of the exercises the designated negotiators had only minimal training or none at all. The exercises were to provide a realistic setting in which they could appreciate the complexity of their new responsibilities. Perhaps fully trained negotiators would not act in the same manner as the newly designated ones did. That contention loses some of its validity when one considers that most negotiation training programs currently do not put their personnel into a realistic setting like that in which the negotiators found themselves during the simulations. Thus the reaction of the formally trained negotiator and the newly designated one might differ by degree, but the patterns of behavior displayed by both would still contain similarities. In many departments, even if negotiators have been designated, many of them have received almost no training; their case is similar to the individuals who were assigned their roles as negotiators by the departments and forces participating in the simulations.

At the outset of each simulation it was almost impossible to assess the potential performance of the negotiators. Years of service, rank, and other factors gave no clues about how an individual would perform in the simulations. It was only as the simulations developed that factors indicating good or bad negotiation came to the surface.

In all of the simulations the possibilities for starting an effective dialogue were almost negated at the start of the simulations by the rigidity of the negotiators and the commanders. Valuable time was wasted that might have been spent establishing communication and making small, essentially symbolic gestures to facilitate a degree of trust between terrorist and negotiator. All too often, by their actions and particularly by their inability to listen to the perpetrator, the would-be negotiators immediately created an adversary relationship, which was hardly conducive to the resolution of the incident.

This inability to listen affected negotiators irrespective of age or experience. Authoritarian individuals who were used to giving commands and speaking at, rather than to, people often quickly turned off the hostage-takers. In contrast, in incident after incident where the negotiators could listen, were not disturbed by high levels of verbal abuse, and were flexible and recognized their own limitations, they were effective in developing rapport with the hostage-takers. The implications of those findings are clear: potential negotiators should be put through exercises that are as realistic as possible before training in order to ascertain their capacity to function in their designated role. Such testing is necessary before training because, once he attends a course, an officer may be designated as a specialist simply because he has learned the techniques, although he may not be sensitive to intuitive negotiative skills that cannot be acquired in a short course.

It was particularly vexing in all of the simulations that in the negotiation process so much time was given over to delaying tactics. Opportunities to enter effective negotiation were constantly ignored. For example, opportunities to gather intelligence and exchange hostages for food were often ignored in the command post in an attempt to achieve a total victory over the hostage-takers. This rigidity in part may have been possible because the negotiators were in a highly realistic simulation, but still a simulation, instead of a life-and-death situation. One must question if such rigidity would carry over to an actual incident.

In only one of more than ten simulations was a woman designated to be a negotiator, and even then she was in a secondary role as a log keeper. Males still dominate and form a majority of police and military forces. Also there is some male chauvinism within the law-enforcement community. More female negotiators should be trained, along with members of various ethnic minorities, to be available when the situation warrants it. Terrorism is not a male-oriented phenomenon, and neither should be the training of negotiators.

The Danger of Miscalculation

In the simulations a rise in the level of activity was predictable when it became clear that the siege was reaching a critical phase. The routines that had developed after the early confusion and tension again gave way to high levels of uncertainty in the final stages of the simulation. During this period the following behavior would often occur: at the very time when the crisis was about to be resolved, either by force or by negotiations, the police or military tended to speed up their activities, with potentially disastrous results. Thus, when a course of action based on the use of force was determined to be acceptable, the tactical units that had been waiting in the wings often began to plan and execute the final assault without adequate preparation. It was almost as if the members of the tactical units, after having lived with frustration and boredom as the sieges went on, deliberately mobilized in order to vent their own frustrations at the slow passage of events. Precisely at the time when very systematic measures should have been taken to prepare for the dangers of an assault, preparation often was completed hastily on the assumption that soon the incident would at least end, one way or another.

This temptation to push for a resolution, however dangerous, was also experienced by the negotiators and the commanding officers. Just when negotiation might actually be working, the negotiators often attempted to speed up the action by pressing demands for the resolution of the incident. Again the results were often disastrous. The pressure of the negotiating team coupled with the desire of the tactical team to launch an assault often led to an abortive attack. The experiences of the simulations therefore suggest that it is important for the responding forces to develop a routine and pace themselves throughout the duration of the incident.

The Ignored Victims

Throughout the simulations there was a tendency on the part of the responding forces to get so involved in negotiating with the terrorists and exploring the tactical options that the condition of the hostages was lost in the activity in the command post. In too many instances throughout the exercises the crisis-management team was so concerned with developing a strategy to deal with the hostage-takers that they forgot that the major goal should have been securing the release of the victims. In almost all of the simulations it appeared at times that the only relationship with any importance was the relationship between the police and the terrorists. The hostages were viewed simply as mute and faceless pawns.

This indifference often surfaced at various times during the respective exercises; for example, when hostages were released because of preplanned medical emergencies or breakthroughs in negotiation. Upon release little attention was given to the mental or physical state of the hostage. In some instances, in fact, they were simply ignored. Even more vexing was that in some circumstances the hostages were subject to what amounted to an interrogation by the police or military forces.

While such interrogations were valid to obtain key intelligence information, they were often done without any sensitivity to the feelings of the exhausted hostages. It was almost as if the victims were to blame for their state. It is essential that police and military units know that during and, particularly, after the siege the hostage is only beginning to come to terms with the experience. The following remark by a victim is indeed valid: "Once you are a hostage, you are a hostage for the rest of your life."[1] The responding forces should provide medical and psychological help for the victims because their trauma may continue long after the incident has simply become part of the official log.

Those then are some of the key patterns that emerged at the inception of, during, and at the conclusion of the simulations. Departments confronted with actual incidents might keep those pitfalls in mind, for a miscalculation in an actual incident may be fatal.

17 Conclusion

The various simulations have implications that go beyond the problems encountered by a field unit responding to a terrorist incident involving the seizure of hostages. The response patterns associated with such areas as tactical measures, negotiative positions, and administrative techniques must be viewed in a broader context of policy making at all levels of government. In its most murderous and sophisticated forms contemporary terrorism represents an assault on an entire civil order. It cannot be dismissed as merely a form of criminal behavior or a particularly innovative type of political violence.

The command posts in the simulations were microcosms of critical tension areas. The patterns observed in them are experienced by the policy makers who must prepare for a potential crisis and those who may have to deal with an actual incident in the execution of their everyday responsibilities. The initial disorganization, the working at cross-purposes, the breakdowns in communications, and related characteristics of administrative behavior at the inception of some of the exercises have parallels. They raise serious questions about the ability of administrators and elected officials, who are ultimately charged with protecting the public order, to develop cohesive and effective antiterrorist programs. The terrorists, for their part, continue to work in small, highly flexible strike forces. Increasingly they are coordinating their intelligence and their resources with other groups.

Meanwhile, the responses of senior policy makers at all levels are still fragmented so that the development of consistent policies on the local, state, and national levels is thwarted.[1] The fragmentation carries over into the international area, where cooperation has often fallen victim to the interests of individual nations.

In the United States the fragmentation of effort in part reflects the diversity of the domestic law-enforcement community. There are over twenty thousand law-enforcement agencies on the state and local level and fifty more in the federal government.[2] It is easy to appreciate how the most dedicated policy maker may be frustrated in the attempt to develop an integrated approach to any law-enforcement problem. The unique concerns of each jurisdiction and the differences in style and performance reflect the sensitivity of the agencies to the environments in which

A terrorist captured or killed.

they work, but the differences can act as barriers to effective co-operation. The problem has been partially resolved over the years through some impressive programs to share information and facilities and through the task-force approach. Unfortunately, those programs are meant primarily to be instrumental; they were developed gradually to meet ongoing, relatively long-term problems. An incident of terrorism is often instantaneously multijurisdictional in nature. The selection of targets, the kinds of demands, the tactical environment, and the news coverage may not permit the luxury of a gradualist, integrative approach. There is an immediate need for concerted and unified action at the start of the crisis. It should also be noted that, even if the jurisdictional issue is outwardly resolved by statutes that define the responsibilities of the different agencies involved in a particular kind of incident, lack of coordination may negate even the most well-thought-out plan legislation because of differing interpretations of the operative regulations and conflicts among the different parties to it.

The difficulty of notification and coordination of concerned agencies and other affected parties is aptly illustrated by the problems associated with an aircraft seizure, even when the act is purely domestic in scope. While the Federal Bureau of Investigation bears the prime legal responsibility to take command, a delicate relationship exists between the Bureau as the prime law-enforcement unit and the equally important role of the Federal Aviation Administration, which must provide air traffic control for the affected aircraft in the air and when it enters into flight traffic on the runway. The responsibility may be further diffused at the start of an incident because the regular police force in the local jurisdiction or an airport police unit may have to assume initial command. Finally, the decision-making process, however defined on paper, may be based instead on the judgment of the flight crew in consultation with the airline company's headquarters. While admittedly the seizure of an aircraft brings into play a series of difficult technical problems, it illustrates that, even though there may be legislation on the books to deal with an issue, it is by no means certain that, given the pressure of events, miscalculations will not occur.

A hostage-taking is potentially multijurisdictional. Whether it occurs at a local airport or at the headquarters of a multinational corporation, with or without statutory directives, there is a danger that jurisdictional immobility may prevent the responding units from dealing adequately with a hostage-taking. The deadlocks do not occur only in highly dramatic situations. Lack of coordination among the local police department, the county sheriff's office, and the state police or highway patrol is always a disturbing possibility. Therefore guidelines to deal with multijurisdictional operations should be not only subjected to constant revision but also tested in the most realistic manner possible. The utilization of the simulations technique can clearly be helpful in evaluating and developing a coherent response among involved parties.

The need to test responses and to assist authorities in refining their individual and collective crisis-management techniques cannot be overstated. In the future increasingly sophisticated terrorists may deliberately engage in a form of administrative guerrilla warfare by selecting targets and making demands that pit one responding force against another and neutralize their ability to respond to the threat. In the continuing research agenda for future simulations, there is a concerted attempt to develop new scenarios that immobilize the responding forces' ability to coordinate their efforts and therefore to make countermoves.

The complexities of developing and implementing an antiterrorist policy on the national, much less the international, level go beyond the scope of this book. It must be recognized that, while cooperation within the federal government has been impressive, the difficulty of fashioning a coordinated national response is understandable in the midst of the myriad organizations that have to be consulted both within and outside the government. Certainly there is an on-going liaison among the agencies concerned. Through such instruments as the Office for Combatting Terrorism in the Department of State information is shared and a basic framework for responding to an actual incident has been developed. Beyond that, the difficulty of devising, much less implementing, a national program based on appropriate legislation appears to make such a program a distant and unlikely possibility unless a tragic incident focuses the public's attention on the importance of coordinating a response to an act of terrorism. The unsuccessful attempt to have the Congress act on the ambitious Ribicoff Anti-Terrorist Act as late of 1979 demonstrates that the legislative process will not resolve the broad national policy issues relating to terrorism.[3]

The issues related to developing a national policy will grow more complex in the future. New, and perhaps even more dangerous, forms of terrorism may soon be with us. While overreacting is always a possibility, and such a possibility should be guarded against in a liberal democratic state, the tactics and strategies of modern terrorism are subject to changes that will further strain the capacities of authorities to respond effectively.

Contemporary terrorists have worked increasingly in concert, and they have readily available to them weapons of massive destructiveness. The selection of sophisticated automatic weapons has been extended to include portable hand-held missiles, which have already been used to down civilian airlines. The attacks took place in the airspace over a contested territorial conflict, but an act of aviation terror nonetheless resulted, and such terror can be translated to any flight path. It makes no difference to the victims whether they are flying over a war-torn region or over a peaceful city where terrorists are seeking "to bring the war home" for any number of meaningless reasons. The escalation in the destructive capabilities of the new terrorists offers new disastrous possibilities. For example, the possibility of technologically sophisticated groups resorting to surrogate chemical and biological warfare cannot be dismissed.[4]

As the technology of terrorism changes, so in the long run may the causes. While the traditional justifications may still be used by individuals and groups, we may witness the emergence of a new type of terrorist, the apolitical professional, who selects targets as a means of engaging in exceedingly profitable extortion. There is already a variety of highly vulnerable targets in the multinational corporations and the highly sensitive public utilities. The new mercenaries may choose to act alone or they may act in concert with political groups or nations that wish to apply force indirectly in achieving their goals.

Confronted with the changing threat, simulations are one means by which authorities can learn to deal with terrorism. Such training is essential if we, the potential victims, are to be spared an undeclared war not of our own making.

Appendixes

Appendix 1

Suggestions for Conducting a Simulation

This appendix presents law-enforcement agencies and military units with suggestions for the conduct of a hostage-taking simulation for their personnel. The suggestions are based on an analysis of the exercises discussed in this book. While departments can modify the simulations in order to meet specific training requirements and budgetary and personnel constraints, the following measures should be taken under consideration irrespective of the complexity of the proposed training exercise.

Preliminary Administrative Concerns

In developing the simulation, information about the nature of the exercise, the number of personnel involved, the site, the composition of the terrorist group, and other essential matters should be distributed only on a need-to-know basis. Only individuals who are not going to participate in the simulations should engage in the initial preparation. The information should be withheld from the most senior officers if they are to assume active command during the exercise. While routine requirements make it necessary that command personnel know the dates and times when the exercise is to be conducted, they should be told only that a training program will be under way, not apprised of the kind of operation. Ideally the senior participating staff should be kept totally in the dark about the impending program. To avoid security leaks that could compromise the exercise, only one or two members of the police or military unit should act as liaisons with the individuals who will take on the terrorist roles. It is the function of the liaisons to provide necessary logistical support for those who are going to conduct the operation.

Terrorist Selection

The success or failure of the simulation will depend largely on the capacity of the terrorists to play their roles realistically and pose a credible threat to the responding forces. In order to achieve those purposes a distinctive mix of personnel should be recruited. If possible, individuals with very considerable acting ability and training should compose part of the terrorist group. They should be versed in the techniques of improvisational theater. Because of the discipline required in that kind of performance, an actor will get into his or her role more effectively than an untrained person. Actors know techniques to bring an emotional and physical realism to the exercise that cannot be achieved by untrained personnel. A good simulation requires that the participants do more than intuitively play at being terrorists. Finding such actors and actresses should pose few problems. They can be recruited from local drama departments or community theater groups. The availability of actors and actresses with very considerable talent even in small towns has been a source of constant amazement, and such individuals look forward to the opportunity of performing.

Trained actors cannot provide all the skills required for a credible performance. They must work with others who, because of their backgrounds, can tactically challenge the responding units. The practical sophistication of the exercise will in large part be determined by the training of the participating unit, or units, but certain considerations should be stressed. If the proposed simulation involves an extensive evaluation of the responding special-weapons-and-tactics units, it is advisable to recruit terrorists with a lot of experience in nonconventional warfare. If possible, the terrorists should not be recruited from inside the participating police force, since they then would share the assumptions and values of the policemen whom they would face during the exercise. Distance should be maintained between those who will be taking on the role of terrorists and the members of the responding units. Such detachment enables all of the participants to engage in a more objective post-exercise evaluation. It also reflects the reality that hostage-takers are not part of the law-enforcement community. Recruits can be drawn from a wide variety of sources. For instance, serving members of the U.S. Army Reserves and National Guard may wish to apply their skills as private individuals. That approach avoids the problems of having military personnel serving in their official capacities in joint training with a civilian unit or units. A further inventory of trained personnel can usually be readily acquired by visiting the veterans-affairs offices in a local university or college. It is likely that the office staff will be made up of veterans who know each other's past military careers and the experience of other local veterans. In addition, resource personnel may be drawn from the ROTC units on campus.

Even if the participating departments want a severe test of their tactical capabilities, it is not essential that the terrorist have a great deal of military training. From evaluation of actual incidents and the experience of the simulations it is clear that a dedicated individual or group armed with few weapons and lacking tactical skills can be quite a match for the responding forces if the goal of the police is to free the hostages unharmed. One or two individuals can and have held off the most sophisticated special-operations units.

Whenever possible, minorities and women should be recruited into the terrorist band. Their participation adds a further dimension to the complex relations between authorities and hostage-takers during the exercises. The participation of women, for example, forces the predominately male negotiators to adjust their often-sexist values to a new reality: the women at the other side of the telephone cannot be patronized and may be just as trained and dedicated as their male counterparts. The presence of different ethnic groups is important because it tests the sensitivity of the negotiation teams to the intercultural tensions that can and do develop in actual incidents. The responding forces are also forced to ascertain whether they have personnel who are multilingual and who can relate to the background of the individuals on the other side of the barricade.

Getting Into The Role

Time constraints will largely determine how well the recruited terrorists will get into their roles—an essential process if the hostage-takers are to develop terrorist identities and the necessary motivations to give a credible performance. When time permits, various measures can assist them in assuming their roles. Ideally the potential terrorists should prepare for an assault over a period of weeks so that they can develop group solidarity and a sense of purpose. The process can include the acquisition of "safe" housing and extensive gathering of local intelligence.

Even when preparation must take place in only a few days, it is possible for the terrorists to assume their roles effectively. Each recruit should personalize his revolutionary identity by drawing on his past life and adjusting the facts to the role that he will play in the exercise. Thus in one simulation a woman who had graduated from a university that had been the scene of student-police confrontations was able to fuse that experience into a revolutionary identity. One way of organizing the process is to require each potential hostage-taker to write up his own biographical data as a revolutionary. The same data can be used in evaluating the intelligence capabilities of the responding units.

An additional technique to assist individuals in taking on their roles is the preparation of manifestos that will be issued during the exercises. Such preparation helps the group to develop ideological goals, and the manifestos later challenge the ability of the negotiators and their superiors to respond effectively to the group's underlying motives and subsequent demands. Finally a revolutionary chain of command may be established as the group prepares to go into action. It should be noted, however, that studies of actual incidents and the simulations affirm that new leadership patterns may emerge once an exercise gets underway.

The Intelligence Function

The selection of the target should not be done alone by the terrorist group. It should be based primarily on an evaluation of past incidents in the jurisdiction where the exercise will take place. The threat assessment should be based largely on the perceptions of the officers who must deal with potential strife incidents. It is vital that the terrorists employ the threat assessment in devising their plan of operations since selection of the target must be realistic: The scenario cannot simply be a fantasy. To test the capacity of the officers in charge of intelligence, the biographical data and related information about the terrorist group should be put into the files of the participating departments by the liaison officer. The information should deliberately be incomplete in order to test the analytical abilities of the intelligence staff. Furthermore it should be made available only if the officers responsible execute correctly the processes of collection, evaluation, and dissemination.

Operational Considerations

In the context of the exercise there are two critical areas of concern that should be kept constantly in mind: safety considerations and record keeping for evaluation purposes.

It is essential that at least one officer in the responding unit or units act as safety officer. He or she should ensure that all of the responding forces have no rounds in their weapons at the outset of the simulation, that only designated personnel are permitted to fire blank ammunition from weapons that are correctly equipped with adaptors, and that the firing of those weapons is at such a distance that no one can be burned by a discharge. The officer should also perform a full body search of all those who are to be taken hostage, as a backup to the search that will be conducted by the terrorists. In all the simulations a variety of potentially lethal devices were carried by supposedly unarmed police hostages at the beginning of the exercises.

All of the potential hostages should be informed that under no circumstance should they attempt to gain their release by physical force. They should also be notified that, if there is a medical emergency, it has been preplanned. Consequently, if they fake an illness, it will be assumed that the emergency is real, and it will call for the termination of the simulation. Other than those rules, the hostages are free to act in any way they wish.

In acquiring information for the postexercise evaluation, the following duties should be performed. Log takers should recall all activities at the following sites:

1. In the command post there should be (a) a radio log if not the tape from an automatic recorder, which should be transcribed immediately after the exercise; (b) a detailed log of the negotiations and perhaps other recordings of conversations with the terrorists; and (c) a log of the key decisions made by the command personnel. In the last case it may be advisable to assign a person to recall all of the preparations as well as to keep a chronology of major orders.

2. In a hostage location it is essential to have only two observers: (a) one who records the major moves of the terrorists and (b) one who is in constant contact with an observer outside who monitors the emotional climate in the barricaded area. The latter function is vital in order to reduce tension or, if necessary, suspend a simulation if the atmosphere becomes too heated. Careful monitoring in all of the simulations prevented a suspension from ever taking place because of emotional tension.

It is imperative that the observers maintain a low profile. They should not wear distinguishing badges or bands. Such distinguishing marks can and have detracted from the realism of exercises. Observers should be heard on the radio only when strictly necessary, and, if possible, they should not be seen.

The decision when to end the exercise should be made by the most senior officer of the participating department in consultation with the representatives of other organizations who have personnel in the exercise. It is essential to stress that the outcome—stalemate, successful negotiation, or resort to force—is not the vital consideration: it is the process leading up to the conclusions that serves as a valuable learning experience.

The Evaluation Process

While the extent and the form of the evaluation can differ markedly from one exercise to another, certain basic procedures should be considered. It is advisable that the debriefing immediately after the simulation be very short. All of the individuals will be tired, and only very important remarks should be made. Nonetheless, it is essential that all the participants record their individual impressions of the exercise immediately. In this way they can not only give a fresh account of what took place but also avoid intellectualizing their responses, as is likely to occur if the participants have time to rethink their actions and to compare notes with one another. A full-scale evaluation should be conducted within a day or two after the exercise. At that time all the participants should be encouraged to share their concerns and impressions with one another. Finally an officer should be assigned to do a final report using the logs, the personal impressions, and additional interviews. The report should be submitted to key personnel, such as the tactical team leaders and the negotiators, for final editing before dissemination to the entire force.

Appendix 2

Simulation versus Reality

Common Patterns in a Hostage-Taking Exercise and an Actual Skyjacking

By John E. ("Jack") Cunningham and Stephen Sloan

On September 19, 1978, at 13:30 hours twenty-six police officers representing various agencies were disarmed and taken hostage by a well-trained band of terrorists as they boarded a bus in front of the terminal at Portland International Airport in Oregon. In the ensuing seven hours attempts at negotiation were fruitless. Giving in to frustration, other officers initiated an assault aimed at freeing the hostages. The resulting fire ended with the death and wounding of some of the officers and the apprehension of the surviving terrorists.

That was a planned simulation.

On August 22, 1979, at 23:32 the Port of Portland Police were notified that a United Airlines 727 with 112 passengers was hijacked out of San Francisco and was due in Portland at 01:20. In the early morning hours negotiations began and were successfully completed when the lone skyjacker gave himself up.

That was the real thing, and there were no injuries or deaths to anyone.

Both of those incidents tested the capacity of the responding units to deal with crises, but more than the outcome was different in the two cases. The seizure of the police in September was part of a highly realistic exercise under the auspices of the Port of Portland Police Department to train their personnel and other concerned units and sharpen their capacity to respond to an incident. The simulation was part of a seminar on international terrorism conducted by the author under the auspices of the Port of Portland, Oregon, Police on September 19–20, 1978.

Although the exercise and the actual incident involved different situations, and although the FBI in compliance with statutory requirements directed the law-enforcement responses to the skyjacking, common patterns emerged in both the exercise and the real crisis.

The following observations are derived primarily from analysis of a questionnaire distributed to participants immediately after the simulation and a follow-up form given to individuals who were involved in the skyjacking. The analysis indicated problems that will continually challenge those who must respond to threats within their jurisdictions.

At the inception of and during both the simulation and the skyjacking there were perplexing problems in establishing and maintaining effective communications among the responding forces. One of the participants stationed in the command post during the simulation described the problem thus: "Communication was lax. It seemed that information from the field to the command post was not quick enough in getting to the people." Another officer, who was a negotiator in the simulation, indicated that the communications problem was further aggravated by geographical factors: "Communication between negotiators and command post [were] poor due to separation of locations." Problems in the placement of personnel also related to the skyjacking. One of the watch commanders aptly illustrated physical barriers that hamper an effective exchange of information: "Communication between my department and the F.B.I. was poor, mainly from their reluctance to share information. The command post was located in the United Airlines operations center, an area which was not conducive to a program of this nature." The existence of more than one command post caused a watch commander to affirm the need for the "establishment of a command post in a police-controlled environment."

The communications problems were exacerbated by technical breakdowns in both the simulation and the actual incident. Another officer involved in the skyjacking noted the "lack of information due to portable radios losing battery charge and not having enough batteries to change them." A dispatcher added the following: "Poor radio communications between units. Very few people could copy one another on their 'pack' sets. Dispatchers were required to relay information."

The confusion of multiple command posts and the other communication problems were intensified by problems associated with crowd control or ineffective utilization of personnel. One officer, who was assigned the role of runner for the negotiation team during the simulation, made the following point: "There were too many noninvolved persons located in the command center, which made it difficult to inform leaders of negotiations." A similar problem was described by another officer, who noted that during the skyjacking "there were too many people having access to the gates beyond the screening point."

The confused atmosphere created by the presence of too many people was intensified by the understandable efforts of media representatives to cover the events. A press-relations officer involved in the simulation contended that, while there was "confusion," he appreciated the concerns of the press representatives, with whom he had worked for years. As the officer noted, "I know most of the press, I understand where they are coming from, I don't feel like an adversary to them." That view was not shared by an officer present at the actual incident. He voiced the following complaint: "The press people will attempt to go into unauthorized areas. They do not care if they hurt peoples' feelings or endanger people." Moreover, in contrast to the information specialist who was not an adversary of the media, the officer continued, "I felt the press had become the real enemy."

In both the simulation and the actual incident there were problems in coordinating the various responding units. Thus in the simulation a sergeant, who was an observer in the command post, was concerned that the military police participating in the exercise were not effectively utilized. As he noted:

From the beginning of the exercise it seemed as though the civilian authorities completely forgot about the military members who had surrounded the building. Our personnel in the field had no idea as to what personnel were in the area nor what positions they had.

The lack of coordination also led to inefficient use of available personnel throughout the siege. Thus, a negotiator noted the following: "The support services, SERT, bomb squad, etc., were good, but then they were specialists and knew their jobs. They were grossly under utilized and in some cases not used at all."

There were similar problems in establishing command and control over all the agencies that became involved during the skyjacking. As a patrolman wistfully declared, "It would be nice if all the agencies involved could have exchanged information."

This need for sharing of responsibility and for a concerted program to enable all the responding units to work together cohesively was stressed by a Port of Portland policeman, who suggested that his own department should have been given more opportunity to "act in a support-role capacity."

The similar patterns that emerged in both the simulation and the skyjacking reflect the blurred line between reality and fiction in a realistic exercise. As a press-relations officer noted in discussing it, there were similarities in his reaction to the simulation and the actual incident: "[There were] high levels of stress from both incidents owing to the degree of realism achieved in the simulation." This is as it should be, for in the final analysis a simulation can only be effective if it teaches personnel to respond to the tensions that accompany actual incidents. The following observation by an information specialist indicates how proper training can assist the police in resolving a real crisis:

> I felt more prepared for the real incident. I know it sounds questionable, but it's true. The reality of the situation [referring to the skyjacking] . . . as opposed to the unreality of the simulation never struck in any significant way. I was just glad that I'd been able to botch up in a simulation.

Critique

Numerous debriefings and meetings were held with all the participating agencies. As stated earlier, after the simulation and the hijack a detailed questionnaire was analyzed by the Study Group on International Terrorism at the University of Oklahoma. Also, after both the planned simulation and the hijack several procedures were changed:

Communications. The Port of Portland Police Department has purchased from Motorola Communications and Electronics, Inc., a Digital Voice Protection radio system. The system allows police officers to utilize three Port Police frequencies: a frequency on the Port Police radio, a frequency on the Multnomah County Sheriff's Office radio, and an all-talk frequency. This should resolve the problems of establishing and maintaining effective communications among responding agencies.

Command Post. A single police command post has been established after meetings between local and federal agencies. A multipurpose room in the police department has been dedicated for the purpose. With the cooperation of telephone personnel, additional phone lines have been installed. A special call-director telephone with headset is available along with an F.B.I. antenna system. A senior officer from each participating agency is stationed at the command post during a crisis.

Technical Breakdown. Batteries for portable radios have been placed on a constant reorder system. A new battery recharger bank is on order.

Site Access. Access to emergency scenes is limited to working personnel. The Port Police Department has appointed a police media-relations officer who works with the press whenever necessary.

Coordination. Coordination of responding forces is now handled by the senior Port Police supervisor on duty for any incident on Port properties.

Notes

Notes

Preface

1. My concern over these broad issues was incorporated into a paper, "The Functionality of Violence in the New States of Asia and Africa: A Reassessment of Development Theory," delivered at the Annual Meeting of the American Political Science Association, New York City, 1975.

2. For a discussion of the major characteristics of nonterritorial terrorism see *The Anatomy of Non-Territorial Terrorism*, my contribution to the Clandestine Tactics and Technology Series.

3. Stephen Sloan and Richard Kearney, "Non-Territorial Terrorism: An Empirical Approach to Policy Formation," *Conflict: An International Journal of Conflict and Policy Studies* 1(1978):131–44.

4. Ibid., p. 138.

5. For a short account of the Emergency Service Division and the broader questions relating to the training of police to respond effectively to hostage takings, see Frank A. Boltz Jr., "Hostage Confrontation and Rescue," in Robert Kupperman and Darrell Trent, eds., *Terrorism: Threat, Reality, Response*, pp. 393–404.

6. Brian Jenkins, *International Terrorism: A New Mode of Conflict*, California Seminar on Arms Control and Foreign Policy Research Paper no. 48, p. 4.

Chapter 2

1. Carlos Marighella, "Mini Manual of the Urban Guerrilla," an appendix to Robert Moss, *Urban Guerrilla Warfare*, Adelphi Paper no. 79, p. 36.

Chapter 3

1. For a discussion of the complexities associated with attempting to define terrorism, see United Nations, General Assembly, *Report on the Ad Hoc Committee on International Terrorism*, Official Records, 28th session, 28 (A/9028).

2. Jenkins, *International Terrorism*, p. 4.

3. For an insightful study of sectarian assassination in the context of the Ulster tragedy, see Richard Ned Lebow, "The Origins of Sectarian Assassination: The Case of Belfast," *Journal of International Affairs* 32: 43–61 (Spring-Summer, 1978).

4. Interview with Wilford Gibson, then Deputy Assistant Commissioner, A Department (Operations), now Assistant Commissioner of Metropolitan Police, New Scotland Yard, July 20, 1976.

Chapter 4

1. The International Association of Chiefs of Police has developed a program entitled "Protective Services: Meeting the Clandestine Threat" to assist authorities in developing their protective-service training for public and private officials.

2. The simulation was part of the National War College courses "New Forms of Violence—Terrorism" and "Strategies of Negotiation." Norris Smith designed the simulation, and William Wit acted as umpire. The classroom exercise involved the seizure of diplomatic officials and corporate executives in a fictitious Latin-American country. It effectively provided an opportunity for the members of the two classes to refine their crisis-management techniques and negotiative skills.

3. The simulation is presented in a coordinated slide-and-sound presentation that is incorporated into the training program of Braniff flight attendants. The latest program is entitled "Terror at 30,000 Feet" (1978). It is a revision of an earlier program, "Terrorism in Flight" (1977).

4. Two of the simulations were videotaped and shown by network affiliates as regular programs. I wish to thank the network executives and staffs for providing a means by which a broader audience could appreciate the complexities surrounding a terrorist incident. The Portland simulation was incorporated into a four-part program entitled "When Reason is Hostage" and was produced by KWTV (CBS), Channel 9, Oklahoma City. It was filmed and shown in a different form on the evening news of KATU (ABC), Channel 2, Portland, Oregon. The Tulsa exercise was filmed and presented by KTEW (NBC), Channel 2, Tulsa. The program was entitled "Exercise in Terror."

Chapter 6

1. Thus in the Tulsa exercise one of the terrorists, Joel Busby, was a petroleum engineer who could create a credible threat by using his particular skills.

2. The term originated in Norman Hadley, *The Viking Process*, p. 44.

Chapter 8

1. The availability of weapons was brought home to me in a project I conducted in my terrorism seminar. I asked the members of the class to see whether they could go through the motions of acquiring the kinds of weapons commonly used by terrorists groups. My only stipulation was that they were required to equip the group from sources within thirty miles of Norman, the home of the university. One week later individuals proved that they could either buy or acquire M16s, AK47s, grenade launchers, and related equipment with little difficulty. In addition, one of the students could have purchased a Thompson submachine gun in a small town near Norman.

Chapter 10

1. Chief Tom Heggy of the Oklahoma City Police Department. This term is also used by the California Specialized Training Institute in the description of the "Terrorism Course" in the Institute's 1978–79 *Announcement of Courses*.

Chapter 11

1. Robert H. Kupperman and Harvey Smith, "Crisis Management: Some Opportunities," in Kupperman and Trent, eds., *Terrorism: Threat, Reality, Response*, p. 227.

2. Daniel E. Shaffer, "Crisis Management: The Challenge of Executive Kidnapping and Extortion Against Corporations," *FBI Law Enforcement Bulletin* 48 (May 1979):14.

Chapter 12

1. Dick Mulder, "Address Delivered Before the 25th General Assembly of the International Press Institute," Philadelphia, May 10–12, 1976, pp. 2–3.

Chapter 13

1. Frederick J. Hacker, *Crusader, Criminals, Crazies, Terror and Terrorism in Our Time*, p. 107.

2. Peggy Mason, "University Conducts Terrorism Course," *The Sentry*, a newspaper published for Minot Air Force Base, May 5, 1978.

Chapter 14

1. Quoted from the title of Hacker's book, *Crusaders, Criminals, Crazies: Terror and Terrorism in Our Time*.

2. Schlossberg brings a unique set of experiences to his knowledge of hostage behavior. While serving with the New York Police Department he received his Ph.D. in psychology. He therefore very effectively combines a vast range of field experience with academic qualifications.

3. This was part of the curriculum in the Federal Bureau of Investigation school in hostage negotiation that I attended, June 13–15, 1977, at the Robert R. Lester Training Center, Oklahoma City. While such classifications are useful in providing the negotiator with a framework for analysis of the hostage-taker's behavior, the inexperienced negotiator may interpret the classification scheme too literally. There is always the danger of stereotyping the complex behavior patterns that emerge under stress.

4. It has been an unstated policy in some police departments and military units that the tactical solution should be attempted if there is a fatality, but such conventional guidelines break down in the press of events.

5. FBI Negotiation Course Notes.

Chapter 15

1. As a result of our concern over media-police relations, Michael T. McEwen, who was then public-affairs director for the Oklahoma Educational Television Authority, organized "Terrorism: Police and Press Problems Seminar" under the auspices of the Oklahoma Publishing Company. The conference which was held on April 14, 1976 brought together representatives of the print and electronic media, as well as senior law-enforcement officials, in a one-day conference. The proceedings were edited and published in "Terrorism and the Media," a special issue of *Terrorism: An International Journal* 2 (1979). That issue also includes the proceedings of a similar conference conducted under the auspice of the State University of New York, the Institute for Studies in International Terrorism, the State University College at Oneonta, New York, the *Louisville* (Ky.) *Courier Journal*, the *Louisville* (Ky.) *Times*, and the American Jewish Committee.

2. Wayne Singleterry, "Air Piracy Staged in Norman," *Daily Oklahoman*, November 12, 1976.

3. Bob Jansen, "Course Simulates Terrorist Simulation," *Minot* (N.D.) *Daily News*, April 29, 1978.

4. Ibid.

5. Script for the evening news on September 20, 1978, KATU (ABC), Channel 2, Portland.

Chapter 16

1. From an interview with an Israeli passenger who was held captive at Entebbe in Uganda. The interview was part of an excellent documentary entitled *Hostage* produced by the American Broadcasting Company.

Chapter 17

1. For a tightly written analysis of terrorist organizational techniques, see Brooks McClure, *The Dynamics of Terrorism*, Clandestine Tactics and Technology Series.

2. Law Enforcement Assistance Administration, *Criminal Justice Agencies*, p. 1.

3. This act was designed to provide an administrative reorganization to deal with acts of terrorism. It also included a series of sanctions that could be imposed on states supporting terrorist activities. No action has been taken on the proposed bill.

4. For an exceedingly well-written article dealing with these threats, by an author with sound scientific qualifications, see Robert K. Mullen, "Mass Destruction and Terrorism," *Journal of International Affairs* 32 (1978):131–44.

Bibliography

Bibliography

Alexander, Yonah, ed. *International Terrorism: National, Regional and Global Perspectives*. Foreword by Arthur J. Goldberg. New York: AMS Press, 1976.

Alexander, Yonah, and Finger, Seymour Maxwell, eds. *Terrorism: Interdisciplinary Perspectives*. Foreword by Hans J. Morgenthau. New York: John Jay Press, 1977.

Alexander, Yonah, and Kilmarx, Robert A., eds. *Political Terrorism and Business: Threat and Response*. New York: Praeger, 1979.

Bell, J. Bowyer. *Transnational Terror*. Washington, D.C.: American Enterprise Institute for Public Policy Research–Hoover Institution on War, Revolution and Peace, 1975.

Buckley, Alan D., ed. "International Terrorism," special issue of *Journal of International Affairs* 32, no. 1 (Spring–Summer, 1978).

Clutterbuck, Richard. *Guerrillas and Terrorists*. London: Faber and Faber Limited, 1977.

Clutterbuck, Richard. *Living With Terrorism*. New Rochelle: Arlington House Publisher, 1975.

Davidson, Phillip L. *SWAT (Special Weapons and Tactics)*. Springfield, Ill.: Charles C. Thomas, 1979.

Demaris, Ovid. *Brothers in Blood: The International Terrorist Network*. New York: Charles Scribner's Sons, 1977.

Dobson, Christopher, and Payne, Ronald. *Terrorists: Their Weapons, Leaders and Tactics*. New York: Facts on File, 1979.

Hacker, Frederick J., M.D. *Crusaders, Criminals, Crazies: Terror and Terrorism in Our Time*. New York: W. W. Norton, 1976.

Hadley, Norman. *The Viking Process*. New York: Avon Books, 1977.

Hubbard, David G. *The Skyjacker: His Flights of Fantasy*. New York: Macmillan, 1971.

Jackson, Geoffrey. *Surviving the Long Night: An Autobiographical Account of a Political Kidnapping*. New York: The Vanguard Press, 1974.

Jansen, Bob. "Course Simulates Terrorist Simulation." *Minot* (N.D.) *Daily News*, April 29, 1978.

Jenkins, Brian. *Hostage Survival: Some Preliminary Observations*. Santa Monica: The Rand Corporation, April 1976.

Jenkins, Brian. *International Terrorism: A New Mode of Conflict*. California Seminar on Arms Control and Foreign Policy Research Paper, no. 48. Los Angeles: Crescent Publication, Inc., 1975.

Jenkins, Brian, and Johnson, Janera. *International Terrorism: A Chronology, 1968–75*. Santa Monica: The Rand Corporation, 1975.

Kobetz, Richard W., and Cooper, H. H. A. *Target Terrorism: Providing Protective Services*. Gaithersburg, Md.: International Association of Chiefs of Police, 1978.

Kupperman, Robert, and Trent, Darrell, eds. *Terrorism: Threat, Reality, Response*. Foreword by Walter Laqueur. Stanford: Hoover Institution Press, 1979.

Laqueur, Walter, ed. *The Terrorism Reader: A Historical Anthology*. New York: Meridian, 1978.

Law Enforcement Assistance Administration. *Criminal Justice Agencies*. Washington, D.C.: The National Criminal Justice Statistic Service, 1975.

Lebow, Richard Ned. "The Origins of Sectarian Assassination: The Case of Belfast," *Journal of International Affairs* 32:43–61 (Spring-Summer, 1978).

Maher, George F. *Hostage: A Police Approach to a Contemporary Crisis*. Springfield, Ill.: Charles C. Thomas, 1977.

Marighella, Carlos. "Mini Manual of the Urban Guerrilla." An appendix to *Urban Guerrilla Warfare*, by Robert Moss. Adelphi Paper No. 79. London: The International Institute for Strategic Studies, 1971.

Mason, Peggy. "University Conducts Terrorism Course." *The Sentry*, Minot Air Force Base newspaper, May 5, 1978.

McClure, Brooks. *The Dynamics of Terrorism*. Clandestine Tactics and Technology Series. Gaithersburg, Maryland: International Association of Chiefs of Police, 1976.

McEwen, Michael T., and Sloan, Stephen. "Terrorism: Police and Press Problems." In "Terrorism and the Media," a special issue of *Terrorism: An International Journal* 2 (1979), nos. 1 and 2.

McKnight, Gerald. *The Mind of the Terrorist*. London: Michael Joseph, 1974.

Milbank, David L. *International and Transnational Terrorism: Diagnosis and Prognosis*. Washington, D.C.: Central Intelligence Agency, 1976.

Miron, Murry S., and Goldstein, Arnold P. *Hostage*. New York: Pergamon Press, 1979.

Moore, Kenneth C. *Airport, Aircraft and Airline Security*. Los Angeles: Security World Publishing, 1976.

Mulder, Dick. Address delivered before the 25th General Assembly of the International Press Institute. Philadelphia, May 10–12, 1976.

National Advisory Committee on Criminal Justice Standards and Goals. *Disorders and Terrorism: Report of the Task Force on Disorders and Terrorism*. Washington, D.C.: U.S. Government Printing Office, 1976.

National Advisory Committee on Criminal Justice Standards and Goals. *Private Security: Report of the Task Force on Private Security*. Washington, D.C.: U.S. Government Printing Office, 1976.

O'Neill, Bard E. *Armed Struggle in Palestine: A Political-Military Analysis*. Boulder: Westview Press, 1978.

O'Neill, Bard E. *Revolutionary Warfare in the Middle East*. Introduction by General S. L. A. Marshall. Boulder: Paladine Press, 1974.

Parry, Albert. *Terrorism: From Robespierre to Arafat*. New York: The Vanguard Press, 1976.

KATU (ABC). Script for the Portland, Oregon, Evening News, September 20, 1978.

Shaffer, Daniel E. "Crisis Management: The Challenge of Executive Kidnapping and Extortion Against Corporations," *FBI Law Enforcement Bulletin* 48 (May, 1979).

Shultz, Richard, and Sloan, Stephen, eds. *Responding to the Terrorist Threat: Security and Crisis Management*. Elmford, N.Y.: Pergamon Press, 1980.

Singleterry, Wayne. "Air Piracy Staged in Norman," *The Daily Oklahoman*, November 12, 1976.

Sloan, Stephen. *The Anatomy of Non-Territorial Terrorism*. Clandestine Tactics and Technology Series. Gaithersburg, Md.: Bureau of Operations and Research, International Association of Chiefs of Police, 1978.

Sloan, Stephen. "The Functionality of Violence in the New States of Asia and Africa: A Reassessment of Developmental Theory." A paper prepared for delivery at the 1971 Annual Meeting of the American Political Science Association.

Sloan, Stephen. "International Terrorism: Academic Quest, Operational Art and Police Implications," *Journal of International Affairs* 32, no. 1 (Spring–Summer 1978)

Sloan, Stephen. "Simulating Terrorism: From Operational Techniques to Questions of Policy." *International Studies Notes* 5, no. 4 (Winter, 1978).

Sloan, Stephen. *A Study in Political Violence: The Indonesian Experience.* Chicago: Rand McNally and Company, 1971.

Sloan, Stephen, and Kearney, Richard. "An Analysis of a Simulated Terrorist Incident." *The Police Chief* 44, no. 6 (June, 1977).

Sloan, Stephen, and Kearney, Richard. "How Terrorists Can be Stopped." Internationally syndicated by The New York Times Company, November 21, 1976.

Sloan, Stephen, and Kearney, Richard. "Non-Territorial Terrorism: An Empirical Approach to Policy Formation." *Conflict: An International Journal of Conflict and Policy Studies* 1 (1978), nos. 1 and 2.

United Nations General Assembly. *Report on the Ad Hoc Committee on International Terrorism.* Official Records, 28th Session. Supp. No. 28 (A/9028). New York: United Nations, 1973.

Wilkinson, Paul. *Political Terrorism.* New York: John Wiley and Sons, 1974.

Wilkinson, Paul. *Terrorism and the Liberal State.* London: Macmillan, 1977.

Index

Index